PENGUIN BOOKS

THE WILD GARDEN

Angus Wilson was born in the south of England in 1913. A part of his childhood was spent in South Africa, and he was then educated at his brother's school in Sussex, Westminster School and Oxford. He joined the staff of the British Museum Library in 1937. When the war came he helped towards the safe storage of the British Museum treasures before serving the rest of the war in Naval Intelligence. It was while trying to emerge from a period of depression and near-breakdown in 1946 that he began to write short stories, a collection of which, *The Wrong Set*, was published in 1949. This met with immense critical acclaim and was followed a year later by a second collection, *Such Darling Dodos*. In 1952 his short critical study *Emile Zola* was published and was followed in 1953 by his first novel, *Hemlock and After*, one of his best-known works. In 1955 he resigned from the Museum in order to devote his time to writing and in 1963 became a part-time lecturer at the new University of East Anglia in Norwich, subsequently becoming Professor and Public Orator. He was made a CBE in 1968 and knighted in 1980.

His other novels are *Anglo-Saxon Attitudes* (1956), *The Middle Age of Mrs Eliot* (1958), *The Old Men at the Zoo* (1961), *Late Call* (1964), *No Laughing Matter* (1967), *As If By Magic* (1973) and *Setting the World on Fire* (1980). His third volume of short stories, *A Bit Off the Map*, was published in 1957.

Angus Wilson died in 1991. Among the many people who paid tribute to him on his death were Malcolm Bradbury: 'He was brilliant in the real sense of the word. He shone and he was very theatrical. Lectures were packed'; Paul Bailey: 'He was the kindest of men. I am not the only younger writer who is indebted to him'; and Rose Tremain: 'Angus Wilson was a great novelist and a profoundly lovable man.'

ANGUS WILSON

———

THE WILD GARDEN

OR SPEAKING OF WRITING

PENGUIN BOOKS

PENGUIN BOOKS

Published by the Penguin Group
Penguin Books Ltd, 27 Wrights Lane, London W8 5TZ, England
Penguin Books USA Inc., 375 Hudson Street, New York, New York 10014, USA
Penguin Books Australia Ltd, Ringwood, Victoria, Australia
Penguin Books Canada Ltd, 10 Alcorn Avenue, Toronto, Ontario, Canada M4V 3B2
Penguin Books (NZ) Ltd, 182–190 Wairau Road, Auckland 10, New Zealand

Penguin Books Ltd, Registered Offices: Harmondsworth, Middlesex, England

First published in Great Britain by Martin Secker & Warburg Ltd 1963
Published simultaneously in the USA by the University of California Press
Published in Penguin Books 1992
1 3 5 7 9 10 8 6 4 2

Printed in England by Clays Ltd, St Ives plc

For

PERKIN WALKER

THIS BOOK came out of the three Ewing Lectures that I gave at the University of California (Los Angeles) in 1960. The Ewing Lectures are intended to be delivered by writers about the process of creation. I make therefore no apology for the inclusion of much autobiography and of many references to my own work. There is no question, of course, of my attempting any estimation of the value of my own books; I have used them only in order to examine some of the ways in which experience can be transmuted into fiction. In the revival of literary criticism in the last thirty or so years, both in England and in the United States, the war has largely been against the influence of Edwardian belles-lettres, which, though asserting the identical nature of criticism and creation, ended up by being an anaemic neither. Not surprisingly the leading and most effective opposition to such shapelessness and diffusion has been the most exact, the most disciplined, and the most unrelenting branch of criticism – close attention to text, sometimes (is it in affection, or is it in faint mockery of its puritan tendencies?) called 'pure' criticism. There have been rival new approaches, of course, in particular historical or social criticism, and biographical or psychological criticism. Nor has 'pure' criticism always disdained their assistance. Yet the general sense, I think, has been towards suspecting the historical or biographical approach as, if not disreputable like the old belles-lettres, yet somehow muddying, rendering the 'pure' impure.

In so far as textual 'pure' criticism can be confined to the certainties of image counts (excellent, if limited literary critical aids) these suspicions can be upheld. Biographical criticism with its inclination towards psycho-analysis, historical criticism with its affinity to Marxist interpretation, can hardly qualify as scientific any more than psycho-analysis or historical determinism themselves. If such is to be the meaning of 'pure' then they are not 'pure' as literary computers are 'pure'. But such seldom is, or can be, its meaning; more often the underlying (or overt) impulse of 'pure' criticism is moral. The criticism then becomes that assistance to interpretation from an author's life, or from the history of his age, is somehow less perfectly 'good' or 'honest' than rigid confinement to text.

There are many aspects of this objection that are hardly tenable. In some cases it stems from the fact that many of the greatest writers are not susceptible to biographical treatment, because the information available is and always will be too meagre. By such showing Shakespeare and Homer must set our standards (although wild hazard has been even more rife around their blank or near-blank biographies). Great literary works, of course, are larger than their times or authors. We cannot know many of the particular references in *Volpone* or in *Bartholomew Fair*. The one play would seem to survive this test better than the other. But there is really no good reason for not trying to defy time's corrosion, either in the past, where research can assist, or in the present. There is in this 'pure' objection not a little of that moral puritanism which in various ways easily bedevils even the most purely aesthetic English criticism. If, for example, for Roger Fry any non-formal element in painting was impermissible in criticism, he surely gave to this view a moral flavour in itself inconsistent with the idea of the purely aesthetic; to consider the religious impulse of El Greco or the didacticism of Hogarth was made to seem almost morally disreputable. To suspect all sources outside the text in literary criticism suggests a similar confusion. Allied with this confused puritanism is the underlying suggestion that such aids are suspect simply because they may often be easy short-cuts to textual analysis; they make the critical game too simple.

Such prejudices against the use of biography as criticism seem to be quite unacceptable. Yet there are others which are more creditable. It is certainly easy to set up a confused correlative between an author's work and his life, by which something is read into a novel from a biographical fact and the biography is then illumined or extended by interpretation from the novel. Such a process can easily become a vicious circle. It is also true that the use of biography (though less of history) as an aid to literary criticism may encourage a critic's tendency to fantastic interpretation, although no more, I should suppose, than the interpretation of imagery by the 'pure' critics. It must be admitted that a novelist-critic of novels, by the nature of his own experience of novel-making, and by the very inclinations towards novel-making in him, will be attracted to the biographical approach. The novelist-critic for this reason is often suspect to the academic critic. It is with such hopes and such reservations in mind that I have attempted in this book to relate my own life to my work as an example of some of the elucidations that may arise from the method. Neither the scope of the lectures, nor of the book made from them, has allowed me to do more than select various aspects for consideration. To have attempted anything more exhaustive would anyway have invited the criticism of the psycho-analyst as well as of the pure literary critic. It is, all the same, my hope that what follows may have some interest for the psychological investigator of the creative processes as well as for the student of literature.

The book begins with a general consideration of the relation between the pattern of my life and the themes of my writing. From this I have been led on to consideration of particular incidents, characters, places, and recurrent symbols in my life and work; and to some general estimation of the connection between different levels of imagination and different levels of narration.

The general relation of my life to the themes of my work is perhaps more apparent than in many authors, for I started to write at the age of thirty-six and in unconscious response, I believe, to a definite crisis to which my earlier years had steadily moved. I have also, perhaps, been the more conscious of this direct relation, for I have inevitably pondered a good deal on the connection between myself who had no idea of being a writer up to the age of thirty-six and myself who have now become a full-time professional. My original conviction that this was a pure accident – the taking up of a new hobby – has not stood up to closer examination.

I WAS BORN in 1913 on the South Coast of England. My parents were already getting on in years – my father forty-eight, my mother forty-four. If my father had ever known employment one might have spoken of him as in retirement. It was among retired professional people that they found their social circle. I was the youngest of six sons; the nearest in age to me was thirteen years older. My brothers stood as uncles to me, although there were in fact fraternal jealousies and affections that often crossed strangely over the dividing years. My father was of an upper middle class family and of Scots origin. He had inherited in his youth enough money to live without working, although hardly enough to support so large a family. By the time I was born, his income had seriously diminished, as, indeed, had the money which my mother, born of a well-to-do South African family, had contributed. We lived in genteel poverty, somewhat unevenly, for, if my father did not care to work, he was devoted to gambling and the family income fluctuated with his lucky streaks. In my boyhood and adolescence, indeed, financial necessity dictated that we should live in small hotels and boarding-houses, veering from those with names inscribed across their façades in golden letters, through those inscribed but not gilded, to those only bearing a number. The last were, of course, only boarding-houses; and indeed we once sunk to the depths of middle-class shame of a house at which all the boarders ate at one table. Separate tables, however, we usually maintained. All of them my mother enjoined us to call 'private hotels', as we were to speak of our Boulogne holidays as having been passed 'near Le Touquet'.

My father's fabrications were of a less naïve kind, indeed less innocent and more personal. An inveterate borrower, he was learned in the art of invention. Most of this invention was brilliantly *ad hoc* and sometimes ornamented with daring fabrications quite unrelated to his purpose. In general, however, it included along with all its personal claims (for example to sporting feats and records in all fields, or to exceptional sexual prowess) a certain claim of social superiority which was more justified by his past than his present.

In all this my parents, I think, reflected their class. I do not, of course, mean that there was not a majority of the depressed middle class who, from a certain old-fashioned rectitude or from lack of imagination, kept much closer to the truth. But the air of compensation for lost glories by means of fantasy was pervasive, and I believe that I early imbibed a fiction-making atmosphere.

Financial need to drift from hotel to hotel was reinforced by my mother's colonial upbringing which had not allowed her to acquire domestic talents. 'Native servants' in the South African sense were not to be found in England; native English servants were already becoming a luxury for the genteel poor by the nineteen-twenties. The day-to-day social atmosphere of these hotels played a large part in conditioning the mood and setting of my early short stories, but here I am concerned only with the kind of small boy who was growing up in them. For this purpose all I need to convey is the picture of a lonely and spoilt child, learning about the nature of the world from unhappy, pseudo-sophisticated, *déclassé* adults. Such a child inevitably emerges into this world in a panic – a panic for which the only available protection seems to be to please, to make oneself loved: a popularity in its turn that seems only to be attained by charm, by entertaining, by clowning.

Such solitary sensitive boys have been the stuff of novels from Dickens's blacking factory onwards. It may be said that they have paid diminishing artistic returns since that day. I have not capitulated to the temptation to gain a new hearing for my childhood loneliness in my novels – although I must plead guilty to two short stories which I shall refer to later by way of illustration. I shall not try to do so by oblique means in this book. I only note the fragility of charm, sophistication, popularity – although no doubt like all precocious children I must have had many a hater – and, above all, of humorous fantasy as a solid lid for anyone who is sitting on top of an emotional volcano.

School, with its necessarily harsher judgements, might by old-fashioned moralists have been supposed to have killed or cured me. It did neither. After an initial shock, I found that the same weapons could be used to conquer my environment, or at any rate to allow me to go my own way. What had been a small boy's conscious charm could be converted into a clowning that would entertain other schoolboys, less susceptible than hotel adults to the charms of pre-cocity. However, clowning itself was based on imita-tion and mimicry, which had always been the stock-in-trade entertainment of my lively histrionic family. To family and school I owe my fairly high standard of impressionistic mimicry. I have found it my principal natural asset as a writer.

After Westminster school, neither Oxford nor the British Museum Library, to which I went to work as a cataloguer in 1936, did much to make me regard the foundations of my life more closely. In both it was easy enough to get by comfortably so long as one preserved a measure of good manners. The work which I did in those early years at the British Museum Library might have forced me, by the disappointment it caused me, to think a little more deeply. There can be few more unrewarding tasks for the educated man of curiosity than the routine duties of librarianship; while for the higher rungs of bibliography I soon realized that an avid taste for the contents of books was a hindrance, and that the qualities demanded, of patient, exact scholarship, were those I should never possess. To recall my great affection for the British Museum, I must add that in my last years I was deputy to the Superintendent of the Reading Room, a job in which my interest in people and in books were alike happily satisfied. I doubt very much if I should have started writing at all in 1946 if I had already by then been in the Reading Room.

This initial failure of my job to satisfy me might have forced me earlier into a salutary desperation had it been in any other decade than the 'thirties. As it was, the vacuum was filled by left-wing activities. The busy comradeship, the endless political talk of those years did in fact use up the blank time which might otherwise have driven me to think a little more deeply. In addition this left-wing work gave me a certain moral satisfaction which in turn delayed any serious self-analysis. Conscience and intellect indeed both seemed content. As the horror of the war we had all been long expecting drew closer I buried myself more deeply in a small group of contemporaries whom I could rely on to think and feel as I did. We generated with our lively political talk and coterie jokes a somewhat cosy warmth in which I, at any rate, was able to doze off while believing I was living an intense, engaged existence. I must add to this that I was protected from what might have been the healthily shattering effects of falling in love by my over-close, intense affection for my father. I had become his sole companion after my mother's death when I was fifteen. The utter incompatibility of our tastes and interests if anything intensified our possessive affection; and the fact that the rest of my family, with some good reason, disliked him for his failure as a husband and father only made me the more emotionally engaged as 'the only one who understood him'.

The situation, in fact, asked for retribution; or in more rational terms, I had drawn for an unusually insecure pattern of life. Retribution came, security and the lid collapsed. Out of this collapse came, I believe, not only my impulse to write but the broad patterns of what I was to write.

War came, and to me after a couple of years' delay it brought work at a large inter-services organization in the English countryside. I had lived only a little in the country and then in congenial intellectual week-ending; now I was billeted upon a Methodist widow and her daughter. They were as kind as they were sensible, yet their way of life was so remote from mine that we gazed at one another at times as though each had suddenly been confronted with the proof that vegetables could talk. The darkness of England's war-time blackout closed in upon my hostess and me as she reread Bunyan's *Holy War* for the third time that year. Bed was at ten o'clock; drink was a shock that

I was not hard-hearted enough to confront her with; my chain-smoking she accepted by means of greeting my every cigarette with a dry little chapel joke – in those days this meant twenty-five jokes an evening and fifty on Sundays. I ought no doubt to have changed my billet, but I had adapted myself by my accustomed means of winning affection, and I was prepared to exchange everything for cosy warmth. In a country like England of strictly rationed petrol I was marooned almost each night for almost four years. Even a long acquired capacity to use books as an opiate could not entirely banish many hours of self-communing – something quite new to me. And the communings were painful, for in the organization in which I worked by day I was one of some thousands, and I soon learned that the weapons by which I had gained my way in the past were inapplicable to so large a community. I put up a good fight – indeed it still astonishes me that so many adult people responded to my childish methods before I had to give in; but in the end my will was defeated, and this was the more galling because my will was by no means an ill will, on the contrary it was often sensible, very hardworking, and friendly towards others to the point of sentimentality. Such a defeat would have been bad enough, but I also fell really in love for the first time – perhaps my father's death three years before had liberated me – and I painfully learned that I had far too little capacity for anything except demanding in such

a relationship. All this meant much that was unpleasant to think of in the long, dark, Methodist
evenings. Although I suffered from an acute and
hysteric anxiety state I continued to try to win
approval and to gain my wishes by carrying on at
work – an example of an ambiguously desirable
'pluck' learned from my mother that I shall discuss
later. But what matters at this point is that this defeat
finally forced me to rearrange my experience of life in
imaginative terms, to try to make sense by making
fictional patterns.

I did not immediately or consciously find my
solution in writing. The psychotherapist who gave me
much assistance at the height of this crisis did in fact
advise me to write as an occupational therapy, but then
he also asked me to draw my dreams and to collect
wild flowers. I have therefore never been willing to
regard my writing as imposed on me by a witch-
doctor. It is true that I followed out his suggestions at
that time – I was always anxious to appease – and
joined a circle of amateur writers. Some very feeble
stories by other would-be writers were sent to me in
a folder; I was asked to criticize them and to contribute one of my own. My neurotic lethargy made me
unwilling to take so much trouble; while my vanity
was slighted by the poor quality of my fellow-
members' prose. I sent the folder on untouched and
cancelled my subscription to the circle. It was only
two years later, when the war was well over and my

illness seemed at an end, that I sat down, as they say in faith-healing testimonies, and 'just wrote a story one Sunday'. I called it *Raspberry Jam,* it appeared in my first book of short stories, *The Wrong Set*, and was regarded as the most sensational, though not the most satisfactory, story in the collection. The first eight stories in this collection were written on successive week-ends. My friend Robin Ironside, the painter, saw enough talent in them to show them to the editor of *Horizon*, Cyril Connolly. Like many another author it is to him and his then secretary, Sonia Brownell, that I owe my first appearance in print.

My crisis, then, was that of a man thirty-three years old, whose emotional, *ad hoc* plan of living had broken down. I had found myself in a highly organized, competitive assertive community in my war work (many of my colleagues were business men or tough-minded dons disguised in service uniform). In this rat race my tactics proved unavailing; that I believed my motives to be humane and liberal aggravated my disappointment at my failure. On the other hand I had had for the first time to cope with solitude and self-knowledge – and these with that intensity of emotion, both joyous and melancholy, that country surroundings bring to those who have lived most of their lives in towns. In all quarters, with the community, in love, with so-called inanimate nature, I found an impossibility of communication, the more desperate because on all three fronts I glimpsed at moments some coherences that it seemed quite out of my power to rediscover at will.

With this anxious dichotomy went certain subsidiary discoveries. Bathed in the glow of the cosiness of my earlier life, I had always thought of myself as a person of unusual gentleness and a natural liking for other human beings. I now learnt that I could hate intensely, if not for long periods, and that I was capable of cruelty, indeed addicted to it, particularly towards those who attracted me most strongly. Finally I was forced to think that my sophistication, easy sociability and worldly tolerance had been a form of carefully protected ignorance of life that had fooled myself as well as many around me. The panic that had been packed beneath the lid since my childhood at last broke loose. For some years the panic itself so fascinated me that I could do nothing but analyse it: this I suppose to be the nature of most acute anxiety states. I sought to protect my ignorance by many devious means; for example, I had always been, and still am, addicted to the great Victorian novelists, especially to Charles Dickens. The conflicts of the novels of Dickens or Balzac, for example, so frequently clearer on the symbolic under-level than on the surface story level, seem to me to have not only remarkable social and moral insight but also a cosmic significance that is often denied to them by critics. I used always to be very impatient of more fastidious critics who took exception to the melodrama or the sentimentality –

particularly the sentimentality attaching to childish or childlike innocence; these were such small prices to pay for the intensity, the fierceness, of the struggle portrayed. During the time of my mental illness I battled strongly on behalf of the value of this Victorian sentimentality, relishing it rather than making allowance for it as an inadequacy. Reading, as I read then, almost as a drug, has a powerful illusory effect. I have no doubt that I was helping myself to preserve my illusions with the assistance of the falsities of my chosen reading. Nor was I a whit less able to appreciate the irony of Harold Skimpole as I did so.

All these conflicts and self-discoveries, then, were let loose on the November Sunday in 1946 when I wrote my first short story, *Raspberry Jam,* and they have continued to develop and to feed my writing from then onwards.

An analysis of the making of that first short story may suggest some of the ways in which a novelist unconsciously comes to make one moral statement while supposing that he is making another. The story, the first fictional work of my life, was written in feverish excitement in one day. I proposed earlier that the present book should contain no estimation of my own work, but I pause to say that the failure of English masters, at all the schools I attended, to give me any comprehension of the purpose of punctuation is splendidly evident in that story. It tells of a boy of thirteen, the lonely son of conventional, self-centred upper middle class parents in an English village. He has only two friends in the village: two old sisters of gentle birth, now impoverished, drunken and the subject of village scandal. While an adult group at his mother's house gossip about the two old women, ostensibly asking whether they are suitable friends for the boy, Johnnie returns in his mind to the episode that, unknown to his family, has brought his friendship with them to an end, a terrible and traumatic episode for him. The two old women had invited him to tea. When he arrived they were clearly half-tipsy and they plied him with drink. They then brought in a bullfinch – 'the prisoner' – and tortured it to death in front of him. The act, of course, though to the boy it is just an incredible horror, is in fact a culmination of rising paranoia produced in the simple, imaginative, generous old women by the narrow-minded malice, jealousy and frightened detestation that their originality has aroused in the village. The irony is that in their drunken craziness they destroy their friendship with Johnnie which alone gave any natural play to their generosity and childlike imaginative needs, perhaps destroy for ever the innocence of the boy himself.

When I wrote this story I saw the two old women as the embodiment of that saintliness which the mediocrity of the world seeks to destroy; by this reading, their craziness and their destruction of their young friend's peace of mind is not their 'fault' but that of the world which has failed to cherish them. Yet, as I have subsequently thought of the story, I have felt this to be a disturbingly illogical pattern, at variance with the shape of the story as it unfolds. I see now that what the story *says*, as opposed to what I thought I was saying, is that those, who like my old women, seek to retain a childlike (childish) innocence, and in particular a childlike (childish) ignorance, however 'good' their conscious motives, will inevitably destroy themselves and in all probability those they love. It is not insignificant, perhaps, that Johnnie, who at the age of thirteen might reasonably live in a world of childlike (childish) fantasy, is shown, without my realizing it as I wrote, using this fantasy to protect himself from the reality of his parents' demands upon him to grow up – although their conception of growing up, of course, is an inadequate one.

The character was drawn directly from myself as I had been at that age, but I felt only sympathy with my childhood self as I wrote, and did not notice the sting in the tale. Further, the old women, intended to strengthen the concept of childlike (childish) goodness, but really undermining it, were taken from two old women I knew much later in my life, at the age of twenty or so. And with these women, far from successfully creating an imaginative bond, I rather seriously failed to make any *rapport* at all, whereas a brother of mine was beloved by them. This was the brother next to me who at the age of thirteen had endured his nose being put out of joint by my unexpected birth. He was a saintly and exceedingly selfless man, and I only fear that the old ladies' preference for him showed a greater insight than I granted them; for in real life I regarded them not as receptacles of sanctity, but, like the village in the story, thought of them solely as a crazy nuisance, the more crazy since they did not respond to my charms. I seem in fiction to have righted any disappointment I may have felt by making them the intimates of my own starved affections at a much earlier age.

Such falsification in fact, unconscious at the time of writing (I had no conscious memory of the old women and was only vaguely aware that Johnnie came out of myself) suggests the way in which fiction can be constructed out of protective falsehood. The moral truth of the story was still deep in my unconscious; the conscious mind was soothed with fact unconsciously rearranged to propose a more flattering, untrue moral thesis. But the shape of the narrative defies this falsification.

Implicit in this first story also was the observation of the English social scene as it had changed since 1939. This social aspect coloured the larger part of the stories that I wrote for my first two books in 1949 and in 1950. I was struck then by the fact that a mild social revolution had taken place in England overnight, although its novelists had not yet noticed this. Readers and critics alike responded to this aspect of my stories. Indeed it earned me a reputation for being a 'social satirist', which seems to me only an aspect of my writing. The stories had indeed a sort of *à la page* assessment that 'placed' many things in the new English society that had not yet been mapped. I think that I could not have done this if I had not come from a family and a social background that was so essentially a part of the older disappearing England. The very small-scale *rentier* and professional group to which my family belonged had no place in Labour's England and was subsequently to prove the most expendable element of the Tory Party's supporters when the Conservatives began to convert social-welfare England into an affluent opportunity society. My attitude to this social revolution was inevitably ambivalent, my affections often in conflict with my reason; this is reflected in the stories. Yet I doubt if I could have imagined fictions concerning this social change with any intensity, even though the world of my family was condemned by it, had I not myself been forced at that very same moment to make a similar change-over from long preserved childhood ways to some acceptance of an adult world.

Beneath many of these stories, most of which bear a far more social-seeming surface than the first story, *Raspberry Jam*, that I have analysed, there lies the same

attack on the falsity of preserved innocence or
ignorance. This false innocence is embodied in the
heroes and heroines and in all these characters I
believed as I wrote that I was describing true simplicity.
It would be tedious to detail other examples in
addition to the old ladies of *Raspberry Jam,* but for those
interested I would point to Vi, the night club pianist
in *The Wrong Set*, to the young civil servant hero of
Crazy Crowd, and to the haunted lady of *A Little Companion*. I do not, of course, say that the social statement in these satirical short stories is not rightly the
centre of interest. Nor would it be true to say that
the conflict between emotion and reason embodied
in the social aspect of the stories is altered by the
personal conflict that lies behind it – my affection and
dislike for my youthful self about equalled the
affection and dislike I felt for the dodo classes I
described – but I emphasize the personal impulse here
because I know that without it I should not have
written the stories at all, and I also believe that it is
this underlying personal motive which injects into
them the fierceness that is their strength.

A change comes with the title story of my second
book, *Such Darling Dodos*. This story more openly lays
a charge against the preserved innocence of the
genuinely good, but blinkered, left-wing don and his
wife. I had become by then somewhat more conscious
of my hostility to cherished illusions, at any rate in
the political sphere. Yet in a way, too, once more the

attack shifts to a new, deeper, unconscious level. It is clearly in this story no longer possible to judge on a purely social level. If, for the moment, the sympathies of the educated youth of England have swung against the left-wing causes of Priscilla and Robin (ironically at the moment of Labour's triumph at the polls), no reader (and certainly not the writer) can suppose that these causes have become the less worth-while in themselves. This is not, as my earlier satire on the *nouveau pauvre* or the *lumpen-bourgeoisie*, an attack on *false* standards, but an attack on *insufficient* standards. Robin and Priscilla lack some deeper personal convictions, some poetry to illumine them when history has temporarily turned against them. Even so Robin is given a dignity superior (though no more touching, I think) to the 'pluckiness' of the *nouveau pauvre*. Yet in the long run, for all their superior intellect and better morality, my new liberal targets had failed to realize themselves quite as much as the raffish flotsam of *The Wrong Set*. This attack on insufficient good-works liberalism was to be the conscious theme of the play I wrote called *The Mulberry Bush* with an equally dignified target – the Padleys.

Self-realization was to become the theme of all my novels, offering death to Bernard Sands, the hero of *Hemlock and After*; life and release to Gerald Middleton, the hero of *Anglo-Saxon Attitudes*, and to Meg Eliot, the heroine of *The Middle Age of Mrs Eliot*. Of these three central figures I only consciously identified myself with Meg Eliot. I sought to relate her dilemma to my own. Bernard Sands had for the most part imaginary and literary sources; Gerald Middleton at least two originals in real life. The only quality that the three have in common is the concealment from themselves of their ignorance of the shape of their own lives, a concealment which has to be subtle because it must deceive a habit of rigorous self-inquiry and a trained observation of the shape of the lives of other people. They are practising the final hypocrisies of the educated and worldly.

The nervous crisis then gave me the freedom to write, indeed imposed the freedom on me as an obligation; it also provided me with this very theme of liberation by self-realization, by the rejection of cherished innocence. More profound in its effect on me and upon my work, I think, were the circumstances in which the crisis had occurred – the antithesis of communal life, with its stresses of will and failures of communication, and the solitary life, with its stresses of melancholy and its vicious circle of self-blame and self-pity. This theme is adumbrated first in *Hemlock and After* where Bernard Sands, the successful writer, turns from his high project of a writer's country home (itself an Utopian compromise between community and country isolation) to a solitary, brooding self-condemnation. Self-knowledge brings paralysis of the will and he gives up his prosecution of Mrs Curry's criminal group in the belief that his own relations with his family and his boy friends have been so shot through with sadistic elements that he can account himself too little guiltless to judge others. The scene in Leicester Square in which he realizes with desperation his own sadistic nature may appear too sudden a revelation for a man of Bernard's intelligence who has already passed middle age. Yet for a liberal-minded and overt homosexual to find a thrill in the arrest of another homosexual would surely be so traumatic an experience as to bring to a head every sup-pressed guilt and evaded corruption, particularly since he has long been brooding over the insufficiency of his life and his work. Nevertheless, if this climax seems insufficiently prepared it is no doubt because the book is too short. I was still working at the British Museum Library and had not acquired the technique of writing a novel during long divided intervals – indeed I have never acquired it. Yet the dichotomy of the two evils – the hell of a society that has lost the power of com-munication, typified by the gathering at Vardon Hall, and the hell of the neurotic self-communing, typified by the ice-waste fantasies of Ella, and later by Bernard's solitary country walks – is present in the novel. In the novel, too, the peculiarly sweet, seduc-tive qualities which both kinds of hell offer in mocking consolation to human vanity and egoism – a deceptive sweetness which held me tight in its neurotic grip

31

during my mental illness – were already fully present. It only remained to prepare the crisis more carefully to show it as the result of a life pattern.

This I tried to do in *Anglo-Saxon Attitudes*. If the second novel proved a greater success, it was simply, I think, because, having left the British Museum, I had more time to develop Gerald Middleton. I was enabled carefully to plan a technique of flashbacks and word echoes which would show how self-realization and the purging of guilt (or the acceptance of it) are inevitably a long process of re-living traumatic experiences in memory. I was also able for the first time to expand the canvas of the novel, to give it a setting of an imaginary world broad enough in social scale to make Middleton's personal problem seem no abstraction but the centre of 'life' which expands beyond the novel, beyond the reader's view into 'reality'. It is this, I believe, that prevents a moral theme from seeming a 'set piece' or a formal pattern. It is because I wanted to create this sense of 'life' that I have often used sub-plots and other such old-fashioned devices, not out of any partisan commitment to the 'traditional' English novel or out of any belief that a novel should contain a wide variety of 'real life'. Rather it is that the thematic novel, even at its most excellent, say in *Silas Marner* or *L'Etranger*, seems to me somewhat to evade the basic purpose of the novel. Such novels, it is true, make one *feel* what it is to be a miser or a dissociated man, they expand the personal conviction in a way that an essay on the theme could not do. Yet there is still wanting that sense of being fully made alive, of disseminating the moral proposition so completely in a mass of living experience that it is never directly sensed as you read but only apprehended at the end as a result of the life you have shared in the book. This is the real challenge and triumph of the novel and, however excellent, short thematic novels seem to me to evade it.

But apart from the greater spaciousness of *Anglo-Saxon Attitudes*, essential to a novelist who wishes to explore the themes I proposed to myself, I do not think that the novel marks any thematic change from *Hemlock and After*. The central dichotomy is the same; the cocktail parties, Christmas dinners and social functions still represent the hell of the human failure to communicate (a sort of blasphemy against life, mocking a communion feast); here the damned are the social climbers, those wanting to be loved, the unloved women who push people around, the organization men who fall to pieces when they are alone; the solitary walks and the meaningless reveries represent the opposed hell of the maze of self-pity and neurosis. Gerald Middleton is caught for a time in each; but if there is any difference from *Hemlock and After* it is that Gerald leaves the book a happier man, relatively free even if his freedom is bought at the price of accepting irrevocable guilt, accepting his family's hostility, accepting loneliness; whereas Bernard dies in his self-realization. I am inclined to suppose that this small measure of optimism arose from the immediate sense of freedom, of uncharted horizons which possessed me when I put my old ten-to-five life behind me and embarked in early middle age on a new free-lance existence.

Bernard dies, Gerald accepts life. Readers will judge the second novel as more or less genuinely optimistic than the first according to their views of death. I was, however, uncomfortably aware that this underlying moral dichotomy which seemed to me at the centre of life was imposing a sort of greyness, an anonymity upon my central characters – Bernard and Gerald. Poised between the manic world symbolized by cocktail parties and the depressive world symbolized by the long country walk, my two heroes seemed to me sufficiently to typify modern man's tightrope exist-ence. Yet their very non-committal to either hell made them immoderately moderate. The sexual sensuality which I attributed to both of them got sucked down into their flatness so that it seemed not a redeeming delight or a cause for pride as I had intended, but merely an additional burden, perhaps, of life. I tried therefore in *The Middle Age of Mrs Eliot* to divide my two hells. I cast Meg Eliot, the heroine, as someone already unconsciously in the hell of total social commitment; then I stripped her of her identity by her husband's death and the loss of her money, and reduced her to an existence without her

identity; she immediately plunged into the opposite
hell of neurotic despair. In this I now see she repeated,
as Bernard and Gerald had done, my own crisis. Yet
I tried to show her, by her honesty and toughness, as
able to resume life in the world on a level of self-
knowledge, which, if not remarkable, would at least
be sufficient to prevent her from a second collapse;
she had plumbed the depths and had come up
again.

Her brother, on the other hand, superficially more
profound, had really done little more than elevate his
melancholic neurosis into a system of quietism, had
disguised for himself and others a self-indulgent
apartness under the seeming appearance of a disciplined
self-denial. The nursery community that he had
created in the country is a well-intentioned absurdity.
It was perhaps a distrust of such Utopian communities
that had made me add the failure of Vardon Hall as an
afternote to *Hemlock and After*. David, Meg Eliot's
brother, was forced, of course, to rely on others for
his existence, and it was intended as a part of Meg's
final 'savedness' that she refused to indulge his love of
dependence by indulging her own desire to run his
life. He sinks into his self-absorbed melancholic hell;
she resumes 'life', fortified by some powers of self-
communion. I had divided in this book the two
perilous rocks on which I myself had almost foundered.
There were, of course, many additional aspects of life
that were examined in each of these novels, but

fundamentally the same crisis conditioned three novels
of very different content, shape and texture.

So much for the general themes that the crisis of
my life provided for my short stories and early novels.
What of the context in which these themes were
placed, from what part of my life have I taken the
material of my fiction? Often, as in *Raspberry Jam*, the
events from two parts of my life fuse to make one
imaginative whole. I have already suggested, in the
case of this story, why these two episodes should have
been brought together. In these early stories, in any
case, I found material by deliberately surveying my
youth and adolescence, by using the incidents that I
recalled and mingled in order to reflect ironically
upon the position that the middle classes had reached
ten or twenty years later. Typical of such stories is
Saturnalia, a potpourri of hotel types, assembled for
the servants' ball on New Year's Eve 1931. The story
somewhat confounded American critics, since the
idea of a mixed servants' and guests' dance is a typical
product of British class snobbery. American status
snobbery finds, no doubt, other occasions, office
parties for instance, which indeed have become more
typical in an England now more committed to a status
society. I chose 1931 deliberately both for its direct
reflection upon the relations of the classes in the
opening years of the depression, and for its ironic

reflection in contrast with the changed position of
1947 (the year in which it was written) although overtones of the future are present in the story as they
were in 1931.

Nevertheless the stories never came to me by
selection from a past lying open ready as a book from
which to take appropriately didactic selections. Most
of these short stories came from a remembered phrase
or word that in retrospect seemed to have a curiously
ironic ring. For instance, *The Wrong Set* stuck in my
mind because it had been used by a Church of England
dignitary to describe the world in which his daughter,
to his great distress, was moving. As she lived in the
eminently respectable British South Coast town of
Bournemouth, I had been puzzled. But it later emerged
that to his horror she had become friendly with
'Chapel people'. The anecdote and the expression
became a part of the stereotyped private language
which I shared with my friends. There was a legion of
other such phrases and stories which circulated in my
family circle. It was such expressions, with their
ironic overtones transposed into quite other scenes,
in part derived from other areas of my experience and
in part purely imagined, that were the starting-points
of stories. Such established private jokes may be a
very powerful source of imagination, for long use has
made all their overtones familiar. They are, so to
speak, the personal epics from which more sophisticated literature descends. Their dangers, either of a

preserved nursery immaturity, or of a failure to generalize that condemns the work to coterie communication, are obvious. Much of the 'provincialism' of the English novel derives from this, but so also does its strength, its unstated tensions.

The hotel world of my childhood had been the foundation of these early stories. One by-product of this hotel world appears in what seems to many modern critics the neo-Dickensian caricature of my characters, for the inhabitants of those Kensington hotels tended towards the eccentricity that comes with penurious old age. Such a larger-than-life picture of human beings is inevitably the child's one; in my childhood it was in great degree objectively justified. It was certainly reinforced by my days much later as Deputy to the Superintendent of the British Museum Reading Room. But it is not only the scale of many of my characters in the stories that disturbs my readers, it is also the tone of their speech and behaviour. All writers know aspects of life that they take very much for granted, that yet to their readers appear peculiar, special. Of such a kind, I think, is the pervasive raffishness that hangs around many of my earlier stories and novels. It is the more peculiar, or, at any rate, unacceptable to respectable middle-class readers, because these raffish characters lay claim to, indeed can claim purely by class, social positions and ranks that the middle-class reader prefers to associate with less vulgar, less meretricious, more disciplined, more 'responsible' morality. I suspect my experience of a middle class with its skeletons taken from the cupboard and exposed to public exhibition is not so special as people make out. It reveals a truth about the between-the-wars English middle class when the sanctions that made for Victorian hypocrisy had weakened. At any rate it was my experience from my family, which was strongly reinforced by the atmosphere of my hotel childhood.

To this I can directly relate, I think, one of my greatest difficulties of communication. Vulgarities, lack of discrimination, weaknesses, which appear to me widespread and no more than venial beside the real wickedness of life, so disturb and repel readers that they seem unable to exercise charity toward 'such unpleasant characters'. I have noticed that quite discriminating readers have supposed me to have a puritanical revulsion from the human body, because, for example, in my earlier stories some of my characters spit when they talk or suffer from blackheads. It is rather that my strong sensual pleasure in physical beauty makes me acutely aware of whatever diminishes it. I think that such ways of looking at people, of expectation of human behaviour, remain, even though judgements and understanding may mature or change. That I grew up in a world where the discretion with which the English middle classes once disguised their grosser failures had largely broken down through the desperations of genteel poverty has probably given my picture of middle-class life a permanent colouring.

Finally with this hotel life I should connect one of the chief preoccupations of my earlier work, of the short stories. I mean the ambiguous tone, somewhere between satirical and admiring, with which I describe the resistance of many of my middle-class characters, particularly women, to economic and social decline and the empty disappointment of a life that is going downhill. I suppose that this portrayal is deeply embedded in my attitude to my mother, whose life, to say the least, was hard and heartbreaking. This courage, to which the period and class English expression 'pluck' most satisfactorily applied, commanded my deep admiration and compassion; nevertheless it also commanded my irony because it is associated with assumptions of class superiority, and indeed expectations from society, that reveal both an implacable fear and hatred of the poor and a snobbish envy of the rich. If, throughout my childhood, I knew my mother's 'pluck' to be what stood between us and disaster, I also knew it to be the chilling barrier that cut us off from happy communication with others. We could not know the A's because they were common, we must not know the B's because we could not pay back their hospitality. My mother clung to her 'class' as the only sure rock of a shipwrecked existence.

This 'pluck' I met in the greater part of 'the new poor' ladies (as they would have called themselves) that I knew so well in my youth. It is impossible to say how far such a quality càn have a general significance sufficient to make it a subject for serious literature which is not purely social satire. I am inclined to suppose that the social trappings here are enough superficial to allow the underlying emotion to reach a reader unfamiliar with the social scene. However the ambiguities in this moral courage that I had observed as a child affected me enough to become a central theme in my novel *The Middle Age of Mrs Eliot*. Here I have tried to explore the general moral validity of what I have observed in a particular class by making my central characters, Meg Eliot and her brother, conscious critics of their own courage in face of disaster, and by contrasting them with various types of 'plucky' middle-class women of a more conventional, unselfcritical kind. I have also tried to extend my communication by making my heroine as little familiar with the small hotel world which suddenly confronts her as most of my readers must be. Nevertheless I owe the moral theme – can someone be courageous in sudden adversity without bitterness, without losing their compassion, without losing their humanity? – to these hotel ladies, and I believe it to be one rich in overtones. I offer the case as one example of how novelists – even, I suppose, the nineteenth-century giants who could command a far wider social experience in a far more compact society than any of us can hope for now – have to seek means tc generalize and extend the emotions that they know only in more narrow contexts of class or nation.

However, increasingly as I wrote these early short stories, these *aperçus*, derived from the ironies of private language and the disordered philistine middle-class world in which I had spent my youth, began to prove less satisfactory to me, as did the short story form with its snap ending echoing the ironic title. As I have already suggested, my own personal dilemma, the attack upon contented innocence, that unconsciously lay beneath these social stories was sharpening into the conflict between the twin necessary hells of society and solitude to which the blinkered innocence had to awake. This presented itself to me in two main theses, adumbrated in certain short stories, but demanding, I knew, a fuller treatment.

It is clear to me that as my underlying themes developed so my memory was forced to move on to a later section of my past life in order to find the right stimulation. Stories like *Fresh Air Fiend*, *Crazy Crowd* and *Et Dona Ferentes* still challenge blinkered innocence and still satirize the middle classes; but the blinkered innocent is no longer a child, like Johnnie in *Raspberry Jam,* or uneducated like Vi in *The Wrong Set*; he or she is now a more intellectual person although often without self-criticism. On occasion, even, as in what I believe to be my best short story, *A Visit in Bad Taste*, the fake innocence becomes instead a calculated refusal of imaginative compassion: the sister who

42

can find no place for her vulgar ex-convict brother disguises her selfishness neither with false simplicity nor with thoughtless amorality but with deliberation masked as a superior realism, a refusal of sentiment-ality. Yet apart from its move towards a more intelli-gent, cultivated, self-inquiring anti-heroine, this story's theme was not developed in my later writing; perhaps because it was successfully realized in the shorter form.

Et Dona Ferentes and *Fresh Air Fiend* directly pose the evasion of personal relationship by cultivated, liberal-minded people, and also the absurdity of those who think that such delicate situations can be resolved by honest and frank broadsides. This difficulty was to be developed in *Hemlock and After* (where Bernard and Ella Sands represent the two opposite poles) and in *Anglo-Saxon Attitudes* (where Gerald Middleton unites more subtle conceptions of both approaches in a single person). The more complex note of the novels, however, was imposed upon me as I increasingly felt that the depths of this chasm between the liberal intention in personal relationships and its actual failure were to be found neither in falsely innocent evasion (Ingeborg Middleton), nor even in concern with the externals of tolerant acceptance masking a deeper self-deception (as with Bernard Sands), but in the existence side by side of constant intellectual self-inquiry and emotional blindness (Bernard Sands, Gerald Middleton, Meg Eliot); leading me in the end

to the tragic paradox that the self-knowledge necessary
to bridge the chasm is itself the agent of the stultified
will (Simon Carter, the anti-hero of *The Old Men at the
Zoo*). An allied but less fruitful, more simple theme
was adumbrated in *Such Darling Dodos* where liberal
beneficent public activity is contrasted with failure in
private relationships. This was extended in my play,
The Mulberry Bush, some part of the failure of which may
lie in the fact that I had already solved the artistic
presentation of its essential theme at least adequately
in the earlier story. In any case, it is a theme that has
probably been artistically solved once for all by Henrik
Ibsen.

I have said that this new development in my imaginative interest drew its material from a different
phase of my life. The world of my family and of the
small hotels was essentially the world of the comedy
(and of the pathos) of manners. Contrasts of
behaviours, slang, modes and *idées reçues* of the various
older generations of a section of the British middle
class actively in decline, and of the younger generations conscious of this decline, were the points of
interest that the world of my childhood presented to
the aware observer. The strength of the stories I
wrote about them lies perhaps in the deeper, more
sympathetic overtones of wasted talents, lost hopes,
unrealized dreams that I inevitably imparted to a

picture of people I knew so well, a world to which, after all, I owed my existence. But the new themes that were developing could not be adequately fed upon this material. I sought for a more apparently coherent, more self-conscious world of middle-class values – one, perhaps, that I could take more seriously, both in love and hate, than the philistine bourgeoisie; one that would offer both more sympathetic and tougher targets than those 'natural' innocents – drunk majors, 'fast' middle-class ladies, amateur pros (off tarts), sugar daddies of male tarts, and so on – that were my first targets, all people for whom I had emotional sympathy, but no intellectual regard.

I found my new targets – and thus attacked my own fostered innocence more deeply – in the world of cultured, upper middle class supporters of Left Wing causes, the well-to-do Socialists of the 'thirties. It is often said that these people no longer exist in post-war England. I do not believe that this is true, although, of course, the emotional (and just) source of their political allegiance has been removed with the disappearance of gross economic indecency; such as remain show up less in a more affluent and, superficially at any rate, more liberal-minded society. The old pre-war upper middle class Left, however, was a more homogeneous body, although it contained many different strands, and was not, as it is often represented now, a simple offshoot of what is called 'Bloomsbury'. But whatever the road by which they came to the Left, these professional or business families shared many of the same virtues and defects. They had, I realized about 1950 or so, to share both in the triumph and the failure of Welfare England. It had also become quite clear that they were rapidly proving as much out of touch with the new post-war England as the more stupid middle-class 'dodos' I had satirized in the earlier stories; indeed at certain moments they have been more out of touch. I tried now to place this whole middle-class Left world. In doing so I was dealing with a group of people to whom I had more intense intellectual loyalties, and emotional ties less atavistic no doubt, but to all my conscious sense at least as strong as those that bound me to the world of my family. The change, of course, pressed upon me in two ways, as a change of artistic concentration no doubt must do – in the constant presence of the 'idea', of all that generally connected with the strengths and weaknesses of a class dedicated by ethical duty or intellectual belief to bringing about the end of its own supremacy; but far more than the 'idea' was the constant crowding into my memory of the people and places in my life connected with that idea. I found it, in fact, suddenly difficult to remember my childhood, almost impossible not to recall my late adolescence. The progression copied life, for when my mother died in my fifteenth year I sought and in some degree found substitutes for her affections among the mothers of my friends. These families, unconnected but not wholly

dissimilar, differed from my own by being more cultivated, richer, more elegant and, above all, more
liberal politically. It was they who, altered indeed out
of all recognition, became the centre of my attack upon
the deficiencies of a liberal socialism to which I still
give my own moral and cultural allegiance. This attack
reflects my slow and gradual realization of the many
evasions, the failures of imagination and the cold-
nesses of heart, that marred the ideals of the families
of my adoption. It is perhaps a more killing attack than
the blunt sallies of my early stories against the
Kensington of my childhood, but then disillusionment
with an environment one has chosen is more bitter
than the natural and inevitable reaction against the
environment into which one has been born. The
atmosphere of these families (and especially of these
mothers) of my adoption was at its fullest in *Hemlock
and After,* but still hangs over *Anglo-Saxon Attitudes,*
although in the main the characters and incidents of
that novel are more completely touched by fancy and,
where taken from life, come from more various parts
of my experience than in my earlier novel. With my
last volume of short stories, *A Bit Off the Map*, and the
novels that have followed it, the need to regroup the
events of my childhood and adolescence seems to have
been worked out; the themes of my nervous crisis –
the unthroning of innocence, man's two hells – also
reached their climax in *Mrs Eliot* and have given way
to other themes less apparently connected with my

life, or at present still too close to me to yield to my analysis.

If, as I suggest, my early life had been exhausted as a source, I have to ask myself why certain events should apparently have played so little part in my writing. A good example is the death of my mother. In any event a mother's death is important to a son; my mother's death was very sudden, a culmination of her sad life, her strained relations with my father and, above all, happening as it did in a boarding-house which she felt to be a 'social come-down', a culmination of the genteel poverty and loss of privacy that had increasingly made her life miserable. Certainly this was how my brothers saw it and how I saw it at that time. I have tried to rationalize the absence of my mother as a character, and of her death as an incident, from my writing by supposing that this indicates how little important she was to me. Such a conclusion seems to defy all likelihood, and indeed it does not agree with the fact that throughout my life, although I think of her seldom, if I shut my eyes it is usually her image that comes immediately before me. What I have observed, however, in my writing is perhaps more interesting – deaths that are connected with hers occur in three of my stories, none of them part of my attempted major themes, none of them in my novels. The first, *A Story of Historical Interest*, is an almost direct relation of my father's death, in which I have cast myself in the role of a daughter. My relationship to him was emotionally much that of the daughter he would have liked to have had. The father-daughter relationship is more conventionally acceptable to readers. However I was not aware of either of these motives when I transposed the sex. More interesting is the fact that I have transcribed the events exactly as they happened except for setting them in a small hotel with all the attendant humiliations of the propriet- ress's annoyance, legal regulations about dead bodies in hotels and so on. Now my father did not die or even come near to death in a hotel. My mother *did* die in a hotel. My distress at the time of her death, like the heroine's in the story, was aggravated by this circum- stance, by similar humiliations. Removal to hospital to die is, of course, one of the stereotyped horrors of the impoverished middle class. Critics of this story have told me that the hotel scenes seem the most deeply felt, yet I certainly had no sense as I wrote it that I was introducing an episode from my mother's death. Indeed I was mainly concerned with the special distress we suffer when great public events over- shadow our private griefs. My father died as Hitler marched into Prague. My mother's death in early 1929 was too early even to be overshadowed by the economic crisis.

Twice again, I think, my mother's death has entered my work by a side road. Each time it has been masked behind the death of my country landlady of 1949. In the first, a story called *Heart of Elm* included in *Such Darling Dodos,* the incident is mixed with the account I received second-hand of the death of the matron of my school. The story is mainly concerned to contrast the natural acceptance (one might almost say welcome) of the death of an old servant by her mistress, with the overcharged grief of the adolescent children who do not want to grow up. My two fellow-lodgers pointed out to me when the story was published that they, who with considerable changes figured as the two children, were no more, probably less, sentimentally attached to our landlady, and were certainly less concerned to treat her as a surrogate mother than I had been. I had in fact once again unconsciously attributed 'plucky' life-loving acceptance of death to myself as in *A Story of Historical Interest*. When I came to write a second time about the death of this landlady, I did so consciously and with what I have just analysed in my mind. This time the central figure of a television play, *The Stranger*, was a lodger, and his brutal treatment by the old woman's family after her death is shown as a direct result of his carefully fostered innocence. The fiction, being consciously related to the fact, was less indulgent to myself. My landlady's death had something of the same traumatic suddenness for me as my mother's. I opened the door of her cottage one Saturday afternoon to find her lying on the floor in an apoplexy from which she later died. But what strikes me most is the social element by which, in both stories, the deaths are given an extra pathos derived from the ignorance, simplicity and peasant wisdom of the dying woman. This element in *Heart of Elm* is so marked that an American reviewer could compare the story to a satire on the relations of a Southern family with their old negro mammy. My landlady and, to a less degree, my school matron did have exactly these qualities; to herself and to most observers my mother was far from such a person, yet for me, even at fifteen, she had, through her disappointed shabby genteel life, acquired exactly this pathos. The altered social element stands, I feel sure, for those angers and reflections of her own sense of humiliation that I felt on her behalf at her death when the boarding-house proprietress and the other boarders treated it as something faintly demeaning to the name of the hotel.

So much for examples of particular subjects and incidents which seem to derive directly if unconsciously from my life, or of incidents which perhaps were too traumatic even for unconscious use, but appear obliquely in my writings. More curious perhaps is the relation of an author's life to what can be called the atmosphere of his novels, the flavour given to it by recurring subjects, symbols and places.

If, as I suspect, the creation of atmosphere is the

least reasoned, most unconscious and automatic part of a novelist's art, it is likely also to be the most difficult for him to analyse, even when the particular fiction is a completed work of art, removed from his creative process and, as happens with finished works, appearing to be no longer connected with him. For this reason the oddly assorted *milieux*, objects and activities which I have been able to assemble as recurring, or possessing an apparently mysterious stress or significance, in my novels are probably fewer than another reader could detect; indeed some of those I shall describe were brought to my attention by readers or critics. Such associative objects, too, come so easily as I write, play so little part in the conscious planning that precedes the writing of my books, that they remain, even reviewed in tranquillity, obstinately unsusceptible to analysis. Yet this very material which the author's conscious mind rejects is in great degree the most idiosyncratic aspect of his work, and it would seem desirable that he should throw what small light upon it he can, if only by describing its associations with his own life.

I shall start with gardens and flowers. Their recurrence in my work seems particularly to strike readers – indeed, for those unfamiliar with garden flowers, often to irritate them. Some part they play in my fictions is stated in the first short story in my first book, *Fresh Air Fiend* (in the U.S. *Life and Letters*). Miranda Searle, the embittered, neurotic but clever and once

beautiful, aristocratic wife of Professor Searle, uses
her garden as an exercise in thwarted power to decree
that this plant shall be scrapped and that encouraged;
it is also clearly her last desperate attempt at communication, for if she can no longer 'hear' people,
she has a real feeling for the flowers she tyrannizes
over. When I wrote this story I had never gardened,
although it has since become my chief hobby. I had
only one woman friend who was a devoted gardener
at that time (1946). Had I been told then that she
resembled my character Miranda Searle I should have
rejected the idea, and so I think would others who
knew her. Ten years later when my friend died she
had become an unhappy neurotic not so unlike
Miranda Searle. I should not scout the idea that I could
have drawn a character in this apparently prophetic
manner. I have known too many instances of such
apparent prophecy to be sceptical about this aspect
of character creation. Nor do I think that the pheno-
menon defies rational explanation. If a novelist has
the insight to create a character by the fusion of two
or three real people, or by a combination of observation and fancy, it does not seem improbable that he
may be able, in the process of creation, to fore-
shadow in people he knows degenerations or changes
of character that he is not consciously aware of at the
time. In the case of Miranda Searle, I certainly had no
conscious sense of drawing from my friend. The
character seemed to me, as I wrote, a transposition

into quite other circumstances of what I imagined Lady Ottoline Morell to have been, itself something quite imaginary for I never knew her nor at that time had met anyone who knew her. As to the effects on Miranda Searle of her gardening activities, these were to a large extent drawn from what I felt would be the influence, good and bad, that gardening would have on my character should I take it up as a hobby – something which at that time seemed quite out of the question. Yet I must suppose that the character was much more drawn from what my subconscious told me were the hidden qualities of my friend; for little though I may have had her in my conscious mind, she was my principal association in life with the activity I was describing; and this, despite the fact that she did not, like Miranda Searle, exhibit her desperate possessiveness in her gardening, but found in it her only release from the tensions of her egoistic desperately willed life.

Ella, the principal woman character of *Hemlock and After*, the neurotic wife of Bernard Sands, is also a gardener who has sought refuge from life in her activity. Ella's obsessive fantasies about icebergs and vast stretches of water were taken from my own experience during the period of my acute anxiety state. During that time I also often thought of gardening as a refuge from my fears, as a sort of therapy, but I had not the will and energy to carry through what would in any case have been a difficult scheme. Yet my gardening friend was more closely in my mind when I invented Ella, in certain mannerisms of speech, and in her over-certain dogmatism about moral issues. This certainty, always treated somewhat ironically in the book, is particularly satirized in a conversation with Bernard in which, characteristic- ally, he quizzes her about her dogmatic classification of flowers and weeds. This classification foreshadows her actions after Bernard's death, when she sets to and secures justice against Mrs Curry and her gang, justice which is shown to be ludicrously unsuccessful in its results.

Gardening, then, at this stage of my writing, when I was drawing from observation and not practice, is associated with dogmatic assertion of personal judge- ments, acceptance of too easy definitions of good and evil; it is the resort of the egoist whose will has been thwarted in the field of human relationships (although, of course, I make it clear that both Miranda and Ella deserve much sympathy for the way life has trampled upon their egoistic personalities). Yet with all this there goes a suggestion that association with garden flowers has a certain healing power, however ambig- uous the ethics of gardening. This, I can see, derives from a deep excitement that I had felt from childhood about garden flowers, whose general flamboyance of colour and form had always roused me, where wild flowers left me largely untouched – a taste that, I think, was increased by my childhood period in

South Africa, where both wild and cultivated flowers make an intense battery upon the senses with their colours. The values are conflicting.

By the time I came to write *Anglo-Saxon Attitudes* I had already resigned from the British Museum and was living (on a temporary monthly tenancy) in the country. Would country life be the best background for my new life as full-time writer? One of the chief attractions was the garden, but my decision had to be made on the basis of more directly mercenary considerations, of means of earning an income. I therefore (only partly consciously) temporarily suppressed the internal debate I have just described which was symbolized for me in garden flowers. As a result, although gardening appears in *Anglo-Saxon Attitudes*, it is on a very muted note. Ingeborg Middleton, the central figure's wife, is in character something of a sister to Miranda Searle and Ella Sands. She is, like them, an imaginative, egoistical woman whom upper middle class life, and the ready, automatic selfishness of English upper middle class men, has confined to a pathetically narrow range of hysterical tyranny (but without Miranda's dipsomania or Ella's extreme neurotic disintegration). Automatically I made her a gardener like the other two, yet, unwilling at that time to pursue further the dilemma this symbol posed, I cut down all account of her gardening activities to the minimum, presenting them only as some sort of class badge, like having an account at Harrods or belonging to a golf club. Such class shorthand, satisfactory in short stories, has no place in the portrayal of a major character in a long novel. Ingeborg's gardening in fact is a failed excrescence. I describe the failure only because it is possible that other and better novelists have similarly failed to develop themes because they were, at the immediate moment of writing, sub-consciously unwilling to dwell on them too closely for purely personal practical motives, and yet, by the very pressure of the repression, unable to cut them out altogether from their writing. Such trivial, unworthy immediacies are seldom taken into account in serious literary criticism – they can seldom be known – yet perhaps a close study of biography and works together might avoid weighty and misleading analyses of what is in fact trivial and fleeting.

My uncertainty about country living, and the con-sequent unwillingness to think detailedly about the activity of gardening, persisted when I wrote my next book of short stories, *A Bit Off the Map*, and here too gardening only appears twice somewhat perfunctorily as a class indication. With my next novel, *The Middle Age of Mrs Eliot,* all this was changed. I had accepted the idea of living in the country, at any rate for some years, and I had acknowledged that my garden was the principal pleasure that persuaded me to this important practical decision. Gardens now presented themselves to me as a principal motive in my new novel, but without any very conscious overtones of the internal argument I had laid aside. As a matter of fact, in choosing nursery gardening as the activity of Meg Eliot's brother David and his friend Gordon, I was at first influenced, as in most of my short stories and in all the chapter headings of *Hemlock and After*, by the thought of a pun which would neatly summarize one important aspect of the book's statement. That Meg's living with her brother after her nervous breakdown should be a regression to a cosy and comforting childhood relationship was, I thought, well summarized by the phrase 'Back to the Nursery'. Yet at first the idea of a nursery garden as David's occupation demanded by the pun did not entirely satisfy me; I knew only a little of the working and economics of nursery gardening, and here was a case where I was uneasy in describing or imagining where I did not have some solid background of fact, even if I were never to draw upon it. However, the more I inquired the more suitable the profession seemed for two young men with some private means at their disposal. The habitual internal debate I have described was still not aroused. Yet when the novel's situation came to be worked out in detail, the sympathies (or rather my sympathies, not those attributed to me by the critics) appeared to be very directly marked against gardens, country living and all the values that these symbols implied. David's quietism (though most of the critics thought otherwise) was intended as a final abnegation of life, Meg's refusal to be more than momentarily interested in the nursery garden is intended as a mark of her basic and sane involvement with human concerns.

This contrast, indeed, appears to be a direct rejection of the country life that I had just chosen to live. Yet the rejection, if it is there, was unconscious and could remain so because in the novel it is very curiously hedged about. David's involvement with gardening on a commercial basis is chosen by him very deliberately as a practical background to a contemplative quietist life; the botanical books that he and Gordon write are again deliberately a commercial venture. After the death of Gordon, who for all his faults of egotism and dominance, is committed to living, David's commercially chosen pursuit assumes a more and more routine dead form. If David, as I intended, stands for surrender to sloth, despair of humanity, deliberate destruction of the human will, all under a high-minded self-deception, then his perfunctory use of gardening becomes a characteristic abuse. Indeed it seems to me as I review the book that the nursery, originally chosen for its punning irony, acquires, at any rate in David's hands, a deliberately blasphemous quality, and such force as these scenes have derives, I am sure, from my own unconscious horror at this deliberate and perverse exploitation of nature. It was, without my knowing it, a further step in the internal debate. Or rather not so much a step as a re-wording of the arguments; apparently against gardens because they are associated with David, the plot really speaks for gardens since David abuses their worth. Yet that is not all, for Meg, the real heroine and life force, although she finds refreshment, after her temporary destruction, in gardens (first in the consul's tropical garden at Srempanh, then in her brother's nursery garden), eventually rejects the country. Yet here again the argument is not conclusive, for she also refuses her old metropolitan roots as much as her brother's pretended country ones, and opts for wandering. The debate of town versus country values is sidestepped in favour of vagrancy, or literally perhaps left in the air. At the end of the book she has become an habitual air traveller, although her husband and her happiness had been destroyed in an airport. I had found unconsciously an adequate symbol for adaptation to the modern rapidly changing world. I want to discuss my use of aeroplane travel later. I shall only note here that the tropical garden of *The Middle Age of Mrs Eliot*, indeed the use of the Far East as the scene of Bill Eliot's death and of his wife's ordeal was inspired by my intense impressions of Bangkok shortly before I wrote the novel, though the consul's flower garden recalls a subtropical garden in an early story, *Union Reunion* (1947), which reproduced the South African gardens I remembered from my childhood (very accurately, as a visit to South Africa in 1961 showed me).

Tropical or subtropical gardens, indeed, have

always stood for the 'garden or clearing in the wild' as opposed to the English 'wild garden', a distinction of symbols which lies deep in the dichotomy of values that has troubled me so long. The town-country dichotomy has been central to the English novel from Richardson's time; nor has it been an unfair reflection of the pulls, real and artificial, exerted upon a whole population engaged either in welcoming or rejecting a series of industrial revolutions; or more often attempting to reject and welcome progress at the same time. The contradictions and ambiguities that have collected around both town and country are by now numerous; no person of any subtlety, I believe, can wholly accept either one or the other as 'good' or 'bad'. The 'wild garden' and 'the clearing (or garden) in the wild' which I believe to be at the very root of my symbolic view of life may be of some interest, however, for they represent one man's attempt to resolve this dichotomy of our times, and I have not, at any rate in literature, observed these symbols used in this particular way.

I may begin by regarding them historically. The wild garden, of course, is the eighteenth century's attempt artificially to preserve the noble savage while taming him to fit into elegant surroundings. For its 'sturdy' rejection by the nineteenth century one need go no further than Dickens's malevolent picture of Mrs Skewton craving for 'Swiss cows and china' as she sells her daughter to the highest bidder. But the

Victorian age developed its own version, I think: the pioneer clearing back the jungle, making his plantation on the edge of the wild. Anti-colonialism has shattered this sturdy Victorian image, as Rousseauistic cant sullied the eighteenth-century idyll. Yet both in their way partake of progress *and* of a special sort of nature-worship or primitivism.

In seeking for an imaginative solution for the pressing human dilemma I have been led to both; indeed in my imagination they have become one place, for the wild garden and the clearing or garden in the wild are one and the same place seen from different angles, and they have the great advantages as moral symbols that each claims a completely opposite set of values. If the wild garden seems tame or effete, then the garden in the wild steps in to provide a rough reality; if the garden in the wild seems all colonial pioneer greed and insensitivity, then the wild garden steps in with its elegance, its English absurdity.

The two symbols have become so powerful for me, and, as I shall suggest, lie behind the major themes of my work, because, as I hope to show, they really do have a prelapsarian association for me. They lie in the very earliest conception I ever received of happiness, not even in my own infant happiness, but in the childhood happiness of my mother and my father, unhappy people both, who both looked back from lives of broken-down, failed urbanism to real rural childhood paradises.

My parents, as I have said, were well into middle age when I was born. During my childhood they talked to me a great deal of their early days. In my father's last years this might, although a little uncharitably, have been accounted a premature senility, but by that time I was in my twenties and my attention to his, not always new, stories was at best a means of showing affection. At the time when their tales influenced me in my childhood, they were vigorous middle-aged people. In part I expect their harping upon their childhood was the attempt of ageing people to find a common bond with a beloved but unexpected late child. In greater degree, however, it was the backward-looking talk of disappointed people: my mother disappointed with my father and her sons, both hiding disappointment with themselves in a general disappointment with life.

Almost the only occasions when I sensed happiness in my mother were when she talked of her South African girlhood. She had indeed every reason to wish that she had married one of her many Durban beaux instead of my father, the fascinating Englishman she met on board returning from her first trip 'home' to her grandfather in Lincolnshire. As she talked of her girlhood the sad-eyed, embittered, courageous but snobbish Kensington woman gave way to a curiously gauche, yet flirtatious and, above all, extraordinarily adventurous, hopeful person. When she married my father at the age of twenty in 1889, she must have been a crude, high-hearted, generous, erratic, spoilt and enormously innocent colonial girl. She kept only perhaps her innocence but this, after years of sordid money worries, marital bickering, and brave coping with infidelity, became something that inevitably seemed more like stupidity. It was no wonder that she returned so often to the carefree, tomboy world of rather clumsy practical jokes with her brothers on the mangrove beaches and in the scrub bush of the Island in Durban Bay, or of more violent horseplay with her girl cousins on her uncle's small pineapple plantation a little up-country. The daughter of a well-to-do jeweller who had been an immigrant from Lincoln-shire in the eighteen-fifties, her South African girlhood in the 'seventies and 'eighties must have been a strange mixture of the wild and the genteel. Tomboy pranks in the bush seem to have alternated with the Bee's Wedding on the piano; young men strumming the banjo and singing the 'new' nigger minstrel songs (nothing, of course, to do with the Kaffirs); albums in which it was *de rigeur* for nice colonial girls to answer the question, 'Who would you be if you were not yourself?', with the loyal answer, 'The Queen' (already then in her sixties!); quotations from Long-fellow, Emerson and Tennyson. This English Vic-torianism was reinforced by the young white lady's sacrosanct idleness surrounded by native servants. After a lifetime of make-do-and-mend my mother could still not easily sew and always protested that

her father would have been horrified to see her doing
such native girl's work. And yet, though Durban life
then was correctly genteel and provincial, with small
traces of any pioneer spirit, it had an adventurous air
as my mother looked back on it. The stray hippopotamus that wandered down from Zululand (an incident
that was, to my pleasure, repeated about twenty years
ago), the occasional black mamba in the wardrobe,
the sjambok with which my great-uncle Wakes, the
most 'pioneer' of all my great-uncles, flogged his
daughters even when they were grown to sixteen
years, the threat of massacre in 1879, when my mother
was ten, as the Zulus, victorious at Isandhlwana,
seemed to have a clear road to Durban before them,
all these ran like veins of natural ore through the
artificial gentility of a small tradesman's daughter's
Victorian girlhood. When I came to read *Swiss Family
Robinson* I already had a world in which to set it, the
world of my mother's reminiscence. Although much
of its roughness frightened me (her cousins, it seemed,
glued my mother's eyelids open in a Hallowe'en
prank, they also blistered the soles of her urban feet,
for to their up-country eyes Durban girls were very
much town misses, by making her walk barefoot
through a burnt sugar-cane field), this barbarous
world was lit for me by the radiant light of my
mother's rare moods of carefree happiness. So, I
think, it was that the pioneer garden cut out
of the wild, the 'plantation' petrifying a moment

of primitive beauty became an ideal for me.

When, as a child of nine on my first visit to South Africa, we went to visit my mother's great-uncle Wakes on the pineapple farm where so many of her stories had been laid, I had inevitably peopled it in advance with my dreams. And I was not disappointed. Of course it was not really wild; but Bellair, where he lived, was not then, as now, a mere suburb of Durban. It seemed to me, as a child from southern England, the remote jungle. My great-uncle, blind, with a huge white beard, was more like a pioneer than anyone I had ever seen. Violence, as I had anticipated, was in the air, though a ludicrous pathos, had I been old enough to grasp it, was the keynote of the household. My great-aunt, a tiny ninety-year-old woman, had lost her memory. Their many elderly daughters were cackling like troubled hens because their mother, in her senility, had climbed on to the roof in the night and there had been fired at by her blind husband who had supposed that the intruder must be some 'skellum' native. Luckily, in his blindness, he had failed to shoot her. I listened, agape, to this story, giving me more than all the violence I had expected. My mother, a very histrionic woman, communicated her mood to me, which was one of emotional distress laced heavily with a happy carefree sense of her girlhood about her.

I wandered away on my own into the pineapple fields and there miraculously saw my first mamba (miraculously too suffered no harm from it). *Swiss*

Family Robinson, already familiar reading, was upon me, to say nothing of *Masterman Ready*, another somewhat sententious Victorian favourite. Making my way by back paths to what seemed a remote little outhouse with a stoep (veranda) near the native boys' huts (I was always, to the disgust of my cousins, talking to native servants in their huts) I came upon a sulphur-crested cockatoo in a very old-fashioned cage, and a green parrot chained to a perch. Parrots were almost my 'favourite wild animal', as I should then have phrased it; but they were not unfamiliar to me. My father's stepfather, the very embodiment of bald-headed, monocled Forsyteism, had a grey Amazon in his London flat that drank whisky from a cut-glass dish — it was afterwards said by his second wife to embody his departed spirit and was introduced all round that citadel of Kensington respectability, in Bayley's Hotel, under his name, as it sat upon her shoulder. Another grey parrot, belonging to the care-taker of the block of flats in which we lived at Bexhill when I was a child, had been left with us for some weeks in 1920 and sat on our balcony, recalling the Armistice by repeating over and over again the word 'mufti'. But my great-uncle's cockatoo and green parrot seemed quite remote from such familiar urbanities. I knew enough natural history by then to know that they could have had no native connection with Natal. However, there was a desolate wild air about them, as there was about the whole place, although someone in fact must have fed them. I can only say that at that moment, and always afterwards in my memory, these parrots flew around in a jungle world in which my great-uncle's small plantation was the last civilized clearing. The garden in the wild had materialized and had been fixed for me, and it is for ever bright with my mother's momentary but ecstatically happy recapture of her childhood.

My father's contribution to the symbol was as powerful for me as my mother's. By the time I was conscious of him, my father, at fifty, had become a 'character'. With his nicotine-stained walrus moustache, his Stetson hat or bowler rakishly set on his head, his increasingly roving eye for a pretty girl's legs, his chain-smoking, his anecdotes of real or imaginary past exploits in the West End or on the race track or in Jo'burg, loudly addressed in trains to the assembled passengers, his feverish gambling, his use of 'dear lady' as an address to women, his handkerchief hanging down from his tweed coat pocket like the waiter's in the Phiz drawing for *David Copperfield*, he was taken, I think, as he sat at Simpson's, in the downstairs restaurant (then for men only) eating hunks of Stilton from the end of a knife, or at the Trocadero consuming a whole *omelette surprise* (as he grew older his tastes grew sweeter), for some slightly déclassé late Victorian country gentleman who had come to look like a bookmaker, or some old-fashioned bookmaker who had acquired a touch of the genuine gentleman from his clients. By the time of his death in 1938 he only perhaps still looked at home on the race-course or at Brighton. In his youth he had attended cockfights on islands in the Seine and illegal non-Queensberry-rule boxing bouts. He belonged to the eighteenth-century stream that ran under the Victorian world and emerged as Edwardian. If the wild garden was eighteenth-century he could claim it as my pioneer-bred Victorian mother could the 'garden in the wild'.

If his public character was a bit overbearing, dog-matic and garrulous, a bit, in fact, of an old bore, he had a great deal of charm. His presence for me, particularly when I was a child, usually spelt pleasure, for he spoilt me dotingly. But not always; sometimes he gave way to wild, uncontrolled rages – a behaviour in which almost all my family followed him, so that ours was often a household of shouts, screams, kicking, and objects hurtling through the air. Only as I got older did I understand enough to place these tempers of my father into the regular depressed pattern of his life. I do not know what his ambitions, if any, may have been, or what he had once thought life held for him, but he had only gone for the imme-diate, a life of no work (on a diminishing income, though at twenty-one he could not have guessed that), of games playing, gambling obsessively, whoring rather mildly, at any rate by the time I knew him, and so on and so on. He believed, and he may have been right, that had he possessed sufficient capital it would have been a life of splendour. As it was it had been a life shot through with sordid devices in order to keep going on his own terms – intervals of squalid lodgings in Vauxhall or King's Cross to avoid creditors, money borrowed from racing pals and never returned, money bullied out of women and never repaid, endless tale-spinning to keep the pot boiling. There were long periods when 'luck seemed against him' and then he took to his bed to forget the world; indeed for the last twenty years of his life he seldom found enough point and energy to get up before noon, unless he was going to a cricket match or to the races. The long days were got through in reminiscence of past successes (sporting, amatory or especially of victorious West End fisticuffs in the old Empire parade or with Covent Garden porters). How much truth was involved with fantasy I could not disentangle. When there was no audience he filled in time with reading historical novels, with working out racing form, finally in the last years with muttering complicated money computations of what pathetically ought to have been his, had 'luck' not been against him. He was a generous, attractive, witty, even lovable man, entirely ruined by total self-indulgence. Behind his 'character' manner he was, I believe, usually intensely depressed, sometimes breaking out into anger. His reminiscences, amusing and lively – a whole programme parade in themselves of sporting and West End life in the 'eighties and 'nineties – were yet befogged by a sense of failure, of inferiority that had to be hidden by bluff, of bitterness against life. They were stories of compensating victory in which the other protagonists always exclaimed, 'Well, I don't know how you do it, Billy,' or 'It takes a Willie Wilson to pull that one off.' It was only when he pushed back further still, behind his life as a young man about town with too much (and yet too little) money, back to his childhood, that he could suddenly shed these whole thick accretions of a rather desperate disenchantment and live again with a fresh enjoyment of life. These early reminiscences were all of the country. If my mother had contributed the garden in the wild, my father contributed the wild garden.

It is difficult to disentangle my father's past from the fictions that came to surround it. He was not a socially boastful man, but the implications of his account of his family background had an air about them, and to give him the due he would have wished, I must say that in manner he always lived up to this air. His father's family was Lowland Scots, and if my father was mercifully – unlike my mother – not much given to talk about class, he was a bit free with lore and legend that gave to the Johnstones (our family was proudly hyphenated Johnstone-Wilson) a border foraying disreputability that implied historic lineage. His father he spoke of always rather vaguely as being an officer 'in a good Scottish regiment'. Some of my brothers,

71

who disliked my father, but who yet like all of us were imbued with our parents' snobbery, threw grave doubts on his stories. I think their hostility led them astray and that my father only mildly exaggerated his paternal social background of a small estate sublet into farms, off the rents of which indeed he managed to live for seventy-odd years without working. His detractors were probably on stronger ground in questioning the social origins of his mother. My paternal grandmother was a beautiful woman who ended her days as an exceedingly snobbish, rather vulgar Edwardian Kensington hostess. She always spoke of her father as a diamond merchant; whatever his profession, he lived in the eighteen-sixties in the Haymarket (where my father was born), which, remembering Dostoevsky's lurid accounts of that street in that decade, has always struck me as very odd for a diamond merchant's dwelling. My brothers placed my grandmother as a publican's daughter who caught the Scottish captain on his way through London to Canada where his regiment was sent to put down rebellion.

All this snobbish social chit-chat has its relevance to the 'wild garden' symbol I am trying to describe, for it accounts for a certain ambiguity both in my father's happy childhood reminiscence and in my own imaginative incorporation of it. It was at any rate to this Scottish childhood that my father returned in memory in his sincerely carefree moments – to a childhood spent in a wild garden merging into woodland in Dumfriesshire hill country. If my mother's stories were of mamba and hippo, my father's were of fox and stoat and badgers, and, above all, of ratting (ratting with plenty of blood) – for my father's golden age like my mother's had a good deal of violence that greatly alarmed me as a child. He was a superb teller of stories to small children; for my early diet he invented a raven and with it a whole Scottish wild landscape. Yet all this wild life seemed to be approached, in his stories of his own childhood, from the garden. Years later, in 1929 after my mother died, he took me, a fifteen-year-old boy, to Dumfriesshire to the haunts of his youth. This was his first return to his boyhood home since before his marriage forty years earlier; it was, I'm afraid, a very typical attempt to evade his remorse at his treatment of my mother by going back to his life before he knew her. And indeed why not? Remorse has little value and he was sincerely happy in that trip. I saw then much of the country of small lochs and downland and salmon rivers that had been the background of his youth; but although we were only fifteen miles away we never went to see his old home, which was let, I was told, to some 'retired fellow from the I.C.S.' Perhaps he did not care to chance a regret at what might have been his life. A short while ago, when motoring in Scotland, I went to see the house. To my pleasure its appearance confirmed my father's accounts rather than my brothers' suspicions. There is no doubt an ambiguously snobbish note in my satisfaction that does not only relate to the vindication of my father's veracity. In one particular only did the rather pretty Regency or very early Victorian house set against a background of rolling downland differ from my father's description: the front garden consisted of a neat lawn and a formal shrubbery – nothing could have been more remote from the wild garden I had expected. Perhaps it had been re-styled since my father's childhood, but as an amateur of gardens I doubt it, for the house and its garden are so much of a piece. Perhaps I misunderstood my father, though this again I doubt, for years later my second brother owned a preparatory school with a copse and a wild garden and my father frequently compared it to the playground of his boyhood. Whatever the reality, my father's carefree reminiscence, with its easy acceptance of English wildlife, will always be set for me in a garden that has of purpose been somewhat artificially preserved in its close relation to the wilder countryside around. It stands near and yet in contrast to my mother's garden out of the wild. But the wild garden, as these memories suggest, was far from a purely vegetable Eden. Cockatoos, hippopotami, badgers, and stoats abound. Indeed the animal world has played an even more important part in my imaginative growth. The zoo without bars and the zoological or game reserve have run parallel with the wild garden and the garden in the wild until with my last novel, *The Old Men at the Zoo,* they have entirely taken over.

I realize how closely connected these two sets of symbols are for me when I look back to a conversation that I held with a school-friend when I was about sixteen. We were both in that intellectual stage of applying a very exact rationalism to all the problems we met. My friend proposed the scientific destruction (I think he meant gassing but we had limited scientific knowledge) of all wild beasts as a sensible measure of safety. The suggestion completely horrified me, but, as I clearly remember, the more so because he was a devoted and expert gardener. Gardens and animals are closely connected in my mind.

Young children of all times and places have had an early acquaintance with anthropomorphized animals, first as toys, then in stories ranging from primitive tribal fables to the sophistications of Beatrix Potter. A majority of children nowadays can come to terms with wild life only in books. Many children retain this interest at least into early adolescence, but the interest changes to a fascination with *real* animals, domestic and wild. This is the age for popular natural history books and visits to the Zoo. In the late nineteenth and early twentieth century, and particularly, I think, in Anglo-Saxon countries, stories were written for growing children (primarily middle-class and urban), which in some degree succeeded, although this was not their conscious aim, in bridging the gap between the wolf in sky-blue pantaloons of the young child's book and the real wolves in the forests and mountains. The conscious purpose of these writers – Kipling, Henry Williamson, Jack London, Seton Thompson and many others – in varying degrees, was to impart to children of a domestic, tamed England a sense of the wild and the untamed, or a respect for individual forms of wild life. Nevertheless in doing this they did endow wild animals with human characteristics or feelings – it would perhaps have been impossible, given the earlier anthropomorphic fables, to touch the growing child's fancy in any other way. But the change inevitably was not effected smoothly – the writers were not, had no intention of being, psychotherapists; they were storytellers – there were inevitably ambiguities in the attitude towards wild animals of people brought up, as I was, on this diet. Jemima Puddleduck, Wol, Brer Rabbit, Mr Toad, could be loved (or hated) as people; Baloo and Sheer Khan lie in some uneasy, fabulous realm between animal and human. The White Seal and Rikitikitavi, and even more Tarka the Otter and Salar the Salmon, exist as animals to be identified with; yet for all Mr Henry Williamson's wonderful skill, the otter is not only an otter, not even an otter named Tarka: he is to some extent a person called Tarka who is playing at being an otter. How could it be otherwise really if human fear of strong creatures, or human sense of superiority to weak creatures, were not to be roused in the boys who were being asked to identify with the animals? But the final emotions carried on into adulthood from this reading are inevitably ambiguous.

I have known all these emotions very well. Animals have played an immensely important part in my imaginative world from the earliest age I can remember, and they still do so now. Inevitably they have become incorporated into the dominant debate of my life. I have loved for a very long time animal fables, animal stories, natural history books, above all zoos, and in my adult years I have added some rather amateur reading of animal biology, ecology, classification, etc. *Swiss Family Robinson* was in my childhood years the ideal book, with its concentration of animals of all kinds regardless of geography in one small island. The combination of human mastery of the savage world and pastoral delight in its products soothed a deep sense of chasm that troubled my childhood. Indeed for all its nineteenth-century moralizing *Swiss Family Robinson* belongs to a peculiar kind of eighteenth-century providential pietism, which, despite all its fatuousness, still attracts me greatly, because of its outrageously calm sense of self-sufficiency. Nor was I, as a child, ever averse to the moralizing quality of the Robinsons. The didactic expositions of the peculiarities and beauties of the animal kingdom, in a world hierarchically organized by Providence for Swiss people of Protestant belief, was the most complete and satisfactory resolution of the wild and dangerous and the tame and secure that I have ever known – so long, that is, as I was too young to see its absurdity. I still find it a temporarily comforting book, for it evades all the moral, aesthetic and metaphysical problems of the animal world. Creatures so unabashedly bizarre as the ostrich, the capybara, even the duckbilled platypus are found by the Robinsons, but they offer no cause for awed wonder, only for informative sermons. Animals are killed, it is true, but they do not suffer, either from the Robinsons or from one another, although 'our old sow', if I remember rightly, gets into some trouble from wilder creatures – but this is no more than a rather facetious little family joke (Mr Robinson in his humorous moods is a direct ancestor of Mr Pooter). Animals are tamed and kept in enclosures, but there is no question of any sense of outrage upon the animal kingdom, nor for that matter, of any trusteeship of conservation, for the author lived when wild life still seemed of a perpetual abundance. Finally the Robinsons themselves never seem seriously threatened by the animals, either by direct attack or by the sudden reversion of the tamed. It is an island of primeval innocence, where Fritz may shoot away at his will without causing us a qualm of conscience, for his shots seem no more meaningful than children calling out, 'You're dead!', in Cowboys and Indians. Here indeed was 'the clearing or garden in the wild', as

Mrs Robinson sowed various good Swiss vegetable crops with seeds prudently preserved in her bag. I suspect that it is to this unlikely Eden of *Swiss Family Robinson* that one part of my inner debate is directed.

It was not until my last novel, *The Old Men at the Zoo*, that I made use of this whole animal kingdom symbolism to continue the debate which, in my earlier novels, had been discussed in garden symbolism. Animals had occurred only occasionally in my earlier work, but they have always appeared. Indeed in my very first written work they take the full burden of my discussion of sadism. It is in *Raspberry Jam* that an incident appeared which shocked many readers and critics – the torturing and killing of a bullfinch by the two half-crazy old ladies. Of course I wrote the incident as a shocking one. Yet I also wrote this first short story so fast, in such a tremor of excitement that I had no time to reflect on its significance. Nor was I at that time fully aware of the whole debate which underlay the significance of animals for me. I can only judge of the subconscious shock that the unrecognized blasphemy gave me by the intense excitement I was in when I wrote the episode – an excitement that communicated itself to readers, I think, if I can judge by the strength of their revulsion.

That there was some element of indulgence of my own sadistic feelings I have no doubt. Certainly this

seems to have been the suspicion of critics who talked
about the self-indulgence of the episode; although I
note that such criticism seems likely to reflect some
suppressed desire in the critics too. But since man's
relation to the animal world seems to me of such
importance, I am forced to examine how far the
supposed indulgence of this episode answers to any
overt cruelty, or impulses towards cruelty, to animals
that I can remember in my own life. I can recall that,
as a very small child, like many other children, I was
often barbarously cruel to insects. More disturbing
to me is the recollection that, at as late an age as
fifteen, I deliberately burned moths in the flame of a
candle that lit my bedroom in the seaside house we
rented during the summer holidays. I also remember
clearly that this childish perversity was closely connected with sexual excitement and that the moths were
fairly conscious substitutes for boys at school who had
aroused my lust. Suppressed lusts laced with sadism
are, of course, the commonplaces of English public
school education. Yet I cannot entirely play down the
incident, and I must ask myself how I could so late
have allowed my sadistic impulses to be actually
gratified by a gross abuse of the creature world which
was already then the centre of my most happy sense of
beauty and of hopeful mystery. It is not quite enough
to say, as we all know to be true, 'we needs must hit
the highest when we see it'. I did not, strangely
enough, have any opportunity to gratify my sadistic

feelings at school. It would be a falsity, however, to excuse myself with the plea: better moth-substitutes than actual human flesh and blood; for the question still remains, why anything so lovely and fragile as moths? In asking the question in these words, I see, of course, that I underline the relation to direct sexual desire. Yet at fifteen I was already, in other fields, trying to make, even succeeding in making, some rewarding relationship with animals, plants and the natural world in general. It seems to me, therefore, however much this may rouse a hearty, mocking guffaw, that this aberration may well relate to the anthropomorphizing approach to animals of my childhood, still latent, as I have suggested, in the very books by which I was learning to develop my sense of acceptance of wild life. This reading, in short, had made the substitution of animals for humans in my destructive passions easy for me; as many emotionally deprived people, we are told, can easily sublimate their more harmonious sexual desires in the petting of cats and dogs.

To return to the old ladies and the tortured bullfinch, I see now that my macabre invention was directly related to the old women's innocence which, as I have already suggested, I was consciously defending but unconsciously pillorying. The imaginative games that Johnnie played were only just compatible with his age; even so there was in them a certain conscious clinging to childhood, strengthened by his parents' failure to give him sympathetic understanding. For the old ladies to have so completely shared in such immature games was a pathetic failure to grow up that might surely easily find its outlet in treating a bird as a substitute for human enemies; their revenge has all the nastiness of a young child's (younger than Johnnie) sadistic game. Although I did not recall my burning of the moths when I wrote *Raspberry Jam*, yet it was at the age of fifteen, on that very same summer holiday, that my greatest clash with my parents came over my not growing out of fantasy games similar to those I have attributed to Johnnie in the story. At that time I defended these games because they were shared with my niece, then aged eleven, for whom the games could be said to be far more suitable; yet I knew then that I invented for my own pleasure. My parents were utterly unable to understand me or my fantasies, but this does not of course, as I thought, make these games any the less a tightly clasped refusal to mature. That this battle took place at the same time and on the same holiday as the burning of the moths I have only now remembered some thirty-five years later than the event, but, more importantly, some fifteen years after I wrote the story which embodied them in so disguised a form, attributing the imaginative games to a boy of eleven when I had played them at fifteen, and apportioning my own deliberate cruelty to two persecuted good old women who were only half-responsible for their acts.

This complex concealment of forgotten incidents in life is the more interesting as a sidelight upon the process of conversion to fiction if I add that at the time when I wrote *Raspberry Jam* I had already consciously considered the view that to prolong an anthropomorphizing picture of animals into adult life was one of the principal signs of a hugged immaturity, peculiar perhaps to our own age. Indeed only a month later I embodied this view in a story, *Et Dona Ferentes*. My sympathies in that story were equally divided among the characters; nevertheless the father is more emotionally immature than the rest of his family. 'We have been imagining the badgers drinking in the stream,' said Elizabeth to her father when they returned. 'Is that one of Brock's nightly prowls?' asked Edwin (the father). 'No, darling,' replied Monica, 'not Brock and not nightly prowls. Just badgers drinking. There were rabbits too, but they weren't wearing sky-blue shorts, they were just brown rabbits, with white tails.' Here the wife's attack points out the direct connection between the purely childish view of human-animals with sky-blue shorts and the element of whimsically seen humanity in animals of the more mature boy's reading (Brock belongs very much to the Tarka style of development). Yet my views at that date were clearly not wholly settled, because the story continues: 'Then seeing her husband's hurt expression, she put her hand on his arm. "Never mind, darling," she said. "You like imagining in that whimsical way. I don't; but I think it's only because I don't know how to." '

Of the patronizing and degrading effect of a purely childish sky-blue-shorts approach to animals into adult life I have for some time had no doubt. Mrs Curry, the procuress of *Hemlock and After*, who was intended to stand for all that I hold to be sweetly evil, has a peculiar and quite markedly sexual approach to Walt Disney that perhaps satirizes this whole genre – 'All the little pretty tiny things in those cartoons, the naughty little bunnies in their frillies getting smacked where nature intended, or dear old Pluto catching his nose in the chamber pot.' For me there is a degradation of animals (and consequently, as viewers, of ourselves) in the Disney cartoons, or worse still in the current 'Animaland' where real animals are photographed and their movements and cries fitted to some fatuous story of human behaviour. For instance, to convert the curious lumbering trot of a porcupine to 'Hi, there, Porky, get going,' is vulgar in the most reprehensible sense. It is an approach fairly commonly found in popular commentaries on films of animal life, and not unknown in the commentaries of such excellent naturalists as Mr Peter Scott, who should know better. It seems to me the low point in adult anthropomorphizing of the animal kingdom.

I cannot really find the same corruption in either Lewis Carroll or Beatrix Potter on whose work I was brought up. Perhaps my objection is only a snobbish one to the attribution to animals of certain human class mores that I don't care for; nothing ludicrously sweet or offensively vulgar is to be found in Jeremy Fisher or Mr Tod, and so I am happy with them. Yet it is the great artistry of Beatrix Potter that is more insidious. She is the Jane Austen of English children's literature and, like Jane Austen, makes us accept much that should not be accepted because she is so brilliant.

I can only find three other examples of my attitude to animals in my writing before the whole question of human relations to the animal world became the subject of my novel, *The Old Men at the Zoo*. They relate to different aspects of animals used as instruments to express human mastery and power. The first is in the story, *What Do Hippos Eat* – here Maurice, the pathetic broken-down gent, tries to use the Zoo animals to impress his landlady mistress Greta. His bubble of vanity is pricked by a young cockney Zoo keeper, and burst disastrously and ridiculously in his face in the Hippopotamus House. Here I hope the authentic note is struck by Maurice's comments to a small crowd gathered before the tiger – 'I've only run across this chap's Indian cousin who's altogether smaller fry.' This of the tiger, a creature whose extraordinary beauty, strength and savagery may legitimately excite almost any emotion other than patronage. The whole patronizing behaviour of Maurice and Greta towards the animals is contrasted with the drama student's genuine, if pretentiously worded, admiration of the beauty of the spider monkeys. These monkeys, I see now, are in line with the gibbon in *The Middle Age of Mrs Eliot*, and the lemurs that arouse in Simon Carter, the narrator of *The Old Men at the Zoo,* a near-erotic pleasure – simian grace indeed becomes the exemplar of the beauty of the whole animal kingdom. Gibbons and lemurs (distant though they may be taxonomically) present, I think, somewhat the nearest thing to human grace, as the baboons and the larger anthropoid apes (also somewhat at a distance from one another) seem to caricature human ugliness; and yet they are something so supremely different from the human that they challenge any cosy anthropomorphizing attempts.

Cruelty to animals is treated once again in *Anglo-Saxon Attitudes*, when the Irish layabout kills the baby owl. But here there is no subconscious equivocation as in *Raspberry Jam*. Larrie's squalid sadism is used to underline the weakness of the three adults present who in their varied capitulations to the criminal and *louche* prefer to let him kill the bird cruelly rather than face what he stands for.

Gordon's use of animals in *The Middle Age of Mrs Eliot* to reassure himself of his own power is a more subtle behaviour than Maurice's show-off at the Zoo. Dying of cancer, he has all his pets put to sleep because he cannot trust other people to care for them. Although the incident primarily serves to illustrate the more important character David Parker's priggishly insufficient sympathy, when he criticizes the actions of a beloved friend who is dying agonizingly, yet it is also true that Gordon's capacity to treat his pets as property to dispose of is a mark of a certain ruthless quality in his magnetic personality. It does indeed reflect my own doubts about the orthodox Catholic attitude to animals which separates them so absolutely from the human order by denying them immortal souls – though I have no business to interfere, since I have no belief in such immortality anyway.

All these aspects of the animal world (and indeed of gardening which it replaces) come to a climax in the latest novel I have published, *The Old Men at the Zoo*, in the dilemmas that beset the conscience and paralyse the will of Simon Carter, the narrator – dilemmas which I find insoluble on any but an empirical basis, although they persist in troubling me as being at the root of the contemporary dilemma, the junction point of social ethics and metaphysics.

With the advance of human civilization zoos, or at best natural reserves, may be the only means of preserving wild species for the refreshment, the wonder and the humbling of human spectators; above all, for the instruction of humans in other patterns and rhythms of life, and no less importantly as a recognition and some recompense for our hubris in imposing our will upon the creature world. To a lesser extent gardens may perform the same function for plant species – lesser only in so far as the vegetable world is as yet less threatened. Zoos and wild reserves, botanical gardens, even suburban gardens, need administration, the exercise of power, discrimination. Emotionally I can never feel such discrimination in any sphere – Ella's quick division between weeds to be eliminated and beautiful flowers to be encouraged – to be other than a necessary but distorting corrupting duty. Simon Carter must give his administrative powers to the Zoo, because zoos are needed, may in some years' time be the only means to keep increasingly urbanized man in healing touch with what remains (eventually with a memory) of wild life. He must also administer for the benefit of the animals who give us this refreshment; perhaps, indeed, care for the life of species we are deliberately rendering obsolete by our demands is a paramount decency imposed on men, one which Simon as a competent and humane administrator may most excellently fulfil. On the other hand he can hardly do this job unless he is also an instinctive naturalist, an observer, a watcher, a passive devotee of the wild life that is still with us. Our moment in history demands both forms of activity, and yet they seem so contradictory that inevitably Simon, the administrator, swallows up Simon the naturalist. And, of course, this need at one and the same time for contemplation and social activity, for a secularized form of grace and good works, confronts the humanist as a paradox that can only be imperfectly solved at every level of life.

During the war that overtakes England in the novel Simon is able at last to watch undisturbed the badgers from whose habits and appearance he draws refreshment; but this pleasure which he has so long postponed because of administrative duties, personal loyalties and so on, comes at last only when he must shoot and eat these loved, harmless creatures to save not only himself but two other human beings from death by starvation. The contradictory (and, as it seems to me, inescapable) circle is complete.

The Old Men at the Zoo is the culmination of this inner debate at the time of my writing this book. The Zoo, of course, trying to present its animals in 'natural conditions', is only a new version of the 'wild garden'. The zoological reserve, aiming to freeze the evolutionary battle at some moment of rich variety and pleasing balance, has affinities with the garden cut out of the wild (but as though this had been frozen at a certain moment of pioneer advance). The solution, of course, suggested in these symbols of gardens and wild life reserves is an artificial one, sentimental perhaps, certainly utopian and therefore to some degree absurd. Yet I do not easily see how a resolution of a dualism so vital to civilized man can be other than artificial, or else it would have been long since resolved. It has, of course, been solved for Christians and many other theists by various mythologies of the creation of Eden, but a Lord of Paradise other than man does not convince me. And if the symbolic resolution is an artificial one, it has been so powerful in my imagination that it has not remained purely symbolic. As I shall tell when I discuss the geographical sources of fiction, by an apparent chance when I left the British Museum in 1955 to devote myself whole-time to writing, by an apparent chain of chances I found my home in a clearing in the wild and have since turned it into my permanent home with a wild garden. It will also be apparent later that my subconscious has been fully aware of the fragility of this wild garden symbol, for in *The Old Men at the Zoo* the catastrophic and horrible climax turned out to be at the very centre of my symbolic paradise.

That this traditional English search for roots should have played any part in a writer with my rootless background is perhaps an illustration of the strength of the social form which the universal search for self-identity takes in England. I have suggested that it was to my parents' childhood backgrounds that I was forced to resort in order to find any satisfactory image for the paradise I was searching for; and this is hardly surprising, for since the age of eight I do not remember living in any house or flat for longer than two years. This family vagrancy was inherited by most of my brothers. Three of them at least led almost entirely wandering lives. Even now that I have a house and garden that I own and love, I shudder at the idea of 'being settled'. To my own generation of my *mother*'s family, rich South African business and professional men, a society far from that pioneer 'clearing in the wild' with which I have invested my maternal inheritance, my family – their English cousins – seem probably dubious bohemians as impecunious as we are unrooted, the very stuff of moral wrong in a novel of Jane Austen or Henry James. Indeed when I recently wrote some articles attacking the racial set-up in South Africa, I learned that one of my most established, prosperous cousins had attributed the wrong-headedness of my view to my 'having been brought up in flats'. Yet, despite this vagrant and largely metropolitan existence, the country and its way of life has exercised the old familiar spell upon me that it has done upon most English middle-class authors.

It has not been the rather perfunctory cockney sentimentalism about the countryside of Dickens, who has otherwise influenced me so much, but the much more rooted, cherished and deeply felt attachment of Jane Austen that has shaped my responses. Perhaps this is because London came after childhood patterns had been fixed. I was to live there throughout my adolescence and early manhood, but I have never been a true cockney. My early childhood during the First World War was spent neither in town nor country, but by the seaside where summer mornings on the beach alternated with afternoons catching butterflies or grasshoppers in the lush meadowland that surrounded my father's tennis club. In any case, the sea hardly offers itself as a satisfactory analogy for a rooted way of life, a fixed identity. For me as a child it was either the familiar hardly noticed background to a crab-hunting, rock-pool life of complicated fantasy games, or, very occasionally, a source of terror. Fear of the sea was certainly inculcated in me by the fact that 'across the other side' was the source of all my mother's imparted anxiety over her three sons fighting in France. It was said too, though I doubt this, that the guns could be heard on still days (how ominous a word like 'still' can be in such a context to a child's understanding). I certainly never remember hearing them. Again, set in motion perhaps by the sinking of the *Lusitania*, my mother's reminiscences seemed to encompass every notable story of shipwrecks – particularly, of course, the histrionic story of the *Titanic*, and the sinking of the *Warratah* without trace, I was told, save for the floating body of a little girl in a pink dress. As if all these exotic terrors that attached themselves to the sea at Bexhill in those war years of my childhood had not been enough to make me thalassophobic, I was helped to the panic by the additional disability that I never learned to swim. I have wondered on reflection if this failure to teach a seaside child the elements of self-preservation was due to some wartime emergency regulation against bathing, some danger of mines or what not; but I hardly think so, for although I don't remember once entering the water myself, I can see my sisters-in-law clearly before me dressed in skirted bathing dresses and caps with rubber water-lilies as decoration. I don't remember seeing them in the sea, but since that was not an age of sunbathing I suppose they must have been intent at least on a rollicking splash. The sea was mainly for me a daytime backdrop, occasionally but quite separately a source of fear at night. I don't think that I associated our familiar every-day sea with that which sucked down Mr Astor or the martyred passengers of the *Lusitania* (although I dreamed often enough of that more violent ocean). These night-time fears, perhaps, are the origins of the ice-waste terrors attributed to Ella in *Hemlock and After*. My horror of the Polar seas came early in a picture of Golliwog's head appearing above the ice, entitled 'Golliwog at the North Pole'. And since then I have read all accounts of Polar expeditions – particularly Scott's last voyage – as others may read about psychopathic murders or the horrors of the supernatural.

Despite this close and largely very happy association in childhood with the seashore I found no urge to introduce either sea or shore into my writings save for the story, *Necessity's Child*, which is a near-auto-biography (somewhat self-pityingly set out) of my last childhood seaside years. The alarms associated with the sea did, however, give me great fears of drowning, reasonable fears in view of my inability to swim. When, then, in *The Middle Age of Mrs Eliot* I sought for some vast expanse upon which my heroine could gaze and that would speak to her of the unfamiliar, the escape from her daily persona, alarming yet also alluring, I could not choose the ocean, for its associations for me were all either terror-inspiring or boringly familiar – certainly offering no escape but death. Eventually I decided that it should be in the desert, seen from the air, that Meg Eliot should find the unfamiliar, the element that must destroy her present happiness and yet release her from her hugged cosiness. Air travel indeed ends three of my novels – *Hemlock and After*, *Anglo-Saxon Attitudes* and *The Middle Age of Mrs Eliot* – as the means of escape from that whole group of traditional English dilemmas that I have been describing. The wild garden or the natural reserve stand for resolution of these contradictory demands, air travel stands for escape from them; as indeed it did for me, when after the war I discovered its delights and beauties. I am not consciously any more hopeful of resolving these dilemmas now than I was five years ago, or any the less convinced that by determinedly resisting all the traditional emotional pulls one may in some degree simply escape from them; yet I have to note that in my last novel, *The Old Men at the Zoo*, Simon refuses the only chance of air travel, as an escape from England, which he is offered; the zoo reserves and wild gardens finally come completely into the foreground – attempted resolution has taken over from escape as a symbolic solution. I like to think that this is why Mr Raymond Williams, that honourable escapist critic, in his review found the tone of the book black.

I should also make the point here that when I wrote the passage about Meg Eliot and the desert, it had only been six months before that I had seen the desert myself for the first time, and that from the air. Air travel, too, was comparatively new to me when I wrote the end of *Hemlock and After*. It would be misleading to describe either of these endings as symbols, or rather they are symbols of which not only the author but the characters in the book are fully aware. Such conscious symbols can clearly be taken from quite recent experience. An analogy like the wild garden, however, which is hardly consciously used even by the author, and appears at most by inference from opposites or limitations, is likely to be dredged up from much earlier and more confused levels of memory. What I remember far more clearly than the seashore from the daily routine of my early childhood was the grass and daisy jungle adjoining the tennis-court, in which I did not act out, as on the seashore, fantasy games compounded of anthropomorphized animals, family 'characters' and characters from fiction, but chased butterflies that were no more than butterflies, and grasshoppers or caterpillars that had no fantasy existence for me beyond their strange, natural lives. It was these afternoons, far rosier in memory than the rock-pools and crabs, that form, I have no doubt, the beginnings of my country idyll and, with their more conventional, less imaginative pastimes, fitted easily into the picture I reconstructed from my conventional parents' reminiscences of their childhood. My earliest Eden, in fact, tied in well with the more deeply felt country Edens of my parents.

However, before the countryside could wear anything of this childhood look of enchantment for me again when I came to live in the country in middle age it was to pass through many guises of melancholy and even of fear, which have mixed with the enchantment to create an ambiguous quality in my recollected emotions. This emotional ambivalence matches my rational doubts about the country's adequacy as a pure, ennobling or solid moral force in the lives of responsible, educated, modern men – particularly, perhaps, of Englishmen because its power over them is so peculiarly strong. It is these less happy memories that surrounded country episodes in my earlier tales and novels before 1955 when I became a countryman.

The first country place with which I associate my post-childhood life is my preparatory school; however, as the headmaster and owner of the school was one of my elder brothers, it became also a country home to me right up to 1940 when threatened invasion brought the school to an end. It was not really

a *country* house, for it lay on the edge of Seaford, one
of the more hideous of seaside towns; but it was an
old house, or rather parts of it were very old, and it
had a very large, rambling and very attractive, if
somewhat run-to-seed garden. I associate it much less
with the years when I was at school there than with my
public school and university vacations – long summer
afternoons reading or dozing in a deck-chair to the
perpetual gnawing croak of the rooks that nested in
the copses, or of autumn blackberrying and winter
walks over the Sussex Downs. I was often very happy
there, but nevertheless it is associated with the
melancholies and desperate longings of adolescence.
Indeed, apart from my own emotions, it was a
melancholy, Chekhovian house, for there my family
sat about and talked the hours away like people waiting
for a long overdue train. This train, that in fact never
arrived because the war came first, was total financial
disaster, whose screeching and puffing and whistling
nevertheless often made my poor headmaster brother's
life nightmarish as various members of my family
borrowed his livelihood away. I have reconstructed a
fictitious version of the scene in a story, *Rex Imperator*,
in which my father appears but not my mother. I can
see from this circumstance that I link the house with
the feelings of my late adolescence after her death.
Indeed my brother replaced her in my mythology of
family life as 'the martyr'. But *Rex Imperator*, like
many of my earlier stories, is an objective picture of

a situation I had known, making a double point out of the Tyrant-Victim nature of my brother's relationship to the family.

It seems to me that just such apprehensions of moral ambiguity in relationships should be the stuff of short stories; at any rate, they are of mine. In such a form there is no room for the recall of personal subjective emotion and the story hardly adds therefore to the build-up of 'country' as an ambiguous moral symbol in my work as a whole. A slightly later story (perhaps two months later in composition, but I had been busy writing stories in the interval and was therefore digging deeper) is *Et Dona Ferentes*. The homosexual emotions in this story of a man taken for a ride by a calculating flirtatious Swedish boy are in some part my own at the adolescent period of my life. Unconscious censorship led me to place the story in an imagined Thames Valley setting, yet the original memory asserted itself, for the culmination of the unhappy relationship in the story moves to a downland quite unlike the Thames setting and clearly drawn from the South Downs. Yet here, where my own experience had been deeply compounded with relationships drawn from observation, the melancholic aura of the country scene as I had felt it is absent. This melancholy and despair, however, surround Bernard Sands in *Hemlock and After* when, after the farcical tragedy of the Vardon Hall opening ceremony, he sets off for long solitary country walks.

The scene is set in a neutralized compound of Hert-
fordshire and Buckinghamshire for reasons, which I
shall discuss later, that are revealing of the effects of
the transposition of actual places into fiction. Yet
within this generalized Metro landscape we are
brought up quite suddenly against the Sussex Downs
in a scene which I can clearly recall as being from my
own experience at the age of seventeen.

'He [Bernard] found a great peace far up on a
distant hump of the downs among scabious and trefoil.
There, by the iron railings of a dewpond, he would lie
and gaze into the sky and lose himself for a while in
the hurrying blanket white clouds above him; until
one afternoon he found a solitary duck, swimming in
rapid crazy circles upon the small pond, and instantly
he was reminded of his life with Ella, alone and yet
never alone; and the hill peak, too, became closed to
him.'

I think that, read in its context, the passage does
express the sense of Bernard's pervading guilt for,
run away into solitude as he may, he is for ever recalling
that he has done his wife a great wrong. Such un-
resolved hugged guilt is only just credible as a picture
of the emotions of a clever man of sixty, only perhaps
acceptable if it is considered that, for all his intellectual powers, he has remained emotionally an
adolescent. The emotions in fact were taken from
my own emotions at seventeen. The duck I saw then
on a lonely dewpond somewhere near Firle Beacon

reminded me of what I thought to be my own pitiable isolation in the centre of a philistine, uncaring, yet clinging family. My sentiments were false and self-pitying, as I see them now, but they were perhaps, in fairness to myself at that age, only the rationalizations of an adolescent alarmed by the reality of adult life as it had begun to break through to him. By inserting this particular exact memory into Bernard's general reverie, which in outline was based on other and much later melancholies of my own, I was, I see now, underlining the adolescent quality of his emotional life (openly declared by Ella) and suggesting, what I should not have consciously agreed to as I wrote, that his regrets for his treatment of his wife were no more than regrets for the unhappiness that his failed marriage had brought to himself.

Bernard Sands's melancholy reflections upon the duck in the dewpond, however, have made me digress from the Sussex Downs associations of 'country' in my adolescence. To this world of south Sussex and the wild garden of my brother's pre-paratory school I must add another north Sussex scene – the garden, also partly wild, of the family of one of my closest school and university friends, who lived on the edge of Ashdown Forest. 'Andredas-wood', David Parker's house in *The Middle Age of Mrs Eliot* is, of course, placed in this area. The name is intended to suggest the pretentiousness of David's thinking by its mongrel version of the old Anglo-Saxon name of this area. Yet David's set-up has no connection with the family I knew, could not in fact be more remote from their way of living. The connection is an odd and complex one which may throw light on a novelist's unconscious processes. It was with my friend's family that I first came in touch with gardening as an ardent pursuit; for my friend and his mother at any rate, the garden was the centre of the household existence. This household was more than any other the one in which I found all that my own upbringing had denied me – it was civilized, comfortable, intelligent and so on. Most of my consciously happy times in the nineteen-thirties were spent there.

The central feature, however, of David Parker's nursery in my novel is his use of gardening as a mechanical exercise devised to provide material means on which to live out a deliberately flattened ascetic existence. Since he had once loved gardening, this was a purposeful destruction of that pleasure instinct in himself. I intended it as a mark of the aridity to which his quietism had led him. It was certainly, as I noted earlier in this book, behaviour which shocked my own feeling for the pleasures of gardening, and which attacked the basic symbol lying behind much of my work. Yet in laying Andredaswood geographically where my friend's garden had been, by substituting David's nursery for my friend's loved garden, I was, unconsciously, reproducing David's blasphemy

which I consciously condemned. It is certainly also
the case that only when I had written the book was
I aware that certain superficial traits might connect the
character of David which I so fiercely criticized
(although critics and readers have seen him as my
intended hero) with that of my friend. From this I can
now see clearly what to an outsider might seem
obvious, that my happiness in this surrogate family
was no doubt mixed with a good deal of bitterness
or jealousy which I never allowed myself to realize.
I think that the ambiguity of my attitude to David and
all that he stands for in the novel (an ambiguity clearly
felt by critics, though unrealized by myself) must be
due to this underlying ambiguous memory, especially
since David's sister Meg is in large part modelled on
myself.

This surrogate family's wild garden, however, was
to add another element to the conflicting emotions
with which I came to surround the image. I have said
that my most consciously happy and carefree times
were spent there. I think, however, that in the
nineteen-thirties with their constant, growing menace
of war, 'happiest times' were also those most under-
mined by anxiety and insecurity. From 1936 onwards
to the outbreak of war I do not recall a moment of
happiness which was not shot through with super-
stitious wishes that time should stop and the moment
be held for ever, or, as the complementary negative
of this emotion, another, as it seemed then,

blasphemous, haunting thought that it would be well if time were to be speeded up, the destruction that we saw ahead of us brought upon us – the 'get it over with' instinct that surrounds any too protracted deathbed. (These, of course, are the feelings that possess David as he watches his friend Gordon's slow death.) A good number of the more dramatic moments of that pre-war time came to me in London, in particular the ghastly hysterical days of Godesberg and Munich, for it was in London that I worked and lived. Yet they do not return to me now as the most anxiety-ridden times, for, apart from anything else, I was up to my neck in that most satisfactorily escapist of all activities – busy political work to prevent the coming of war – a world in which the menace did not seem quite real, because it was the current change of all our talk, a world where the terrible wood was never seen for the party political trees. Far more horrible in my memory, for example, is that Easter week-end at my friend's home when the news came of Mussolini's Good Friday invasion of Albania. It was not that any of us were Christians, quite to the contrary. It was not that any of us thought that this was to be the worst or the last of the invasions that preceded war; it was, in fact, one of the last, but we did not know this. No, it was exactly the sense that this threatened happiness might go on and on that seemed most horrible. If I could not have my happiness neat, I would rather that it came to an end. That does not

mean, of course, that I did not at the same time cling
desperately to those happy hours like a drowning man.
I think most of the family shared my feelings; some
clung more desperately to the present, others, hardly
admitting it to themselves, hoped more for an end to
it all, to the doomed paradise.

This doomed paradise, like the sad waiting-room
of my brother's school, is from this time irrevocably
intermixed in my image of the country and of that
special ideal image of the wild garden. This Sussex
house was particularly suited to be connected with
the wild garden symbol, for the layout of the garden
had been made at one time by a German baron who
had built a Swiss chalet in the grounds (associated in
my mind with Rousseau and the whole of his conception of 'nature') and at another by Lady Shelley,
the descendant of Percy Bysshe. As if these historic
associations were not enough, the house, in fact, had
the postal name of 'Wilderness'. Apart from the
unconscious or suppressed hostile association of
this house with the sterile nursery garden of David
Parker in *The Middle Age of Mrs Eliot*, it makes its
appearance once again in *The Mulberry Bush* as the
Oxford College Garden which the Padleys had to
leave. My friend's family were of the Shavian-Fabian
generation, and this in its turn suggests *Heartbreak
House*, Shaw's Chekhovian play in which that earlier
horror, the First World War, descends upon Captain
Shotover's country house idyll. The Padleys are

Fabians driven out not by war but by time and new ideas. The second act contains a number of speeches which, as I wrote them, seemed to belong entirely to the Oxford world I was creating, but which now seem to me to echo the underlying, certainly unexpressed, largely unconscious conflict that in those pre-war days passed between my generation of the young and the middle-aged generation of my friend's parents. By the time (1954) that I came to write *The Mulberry Bush* my generation was itself on the verge of middle age. The youngest generation in the play, Ann and Peter, speak views that represent a rejection of much that my generation believed, yet the emotional overtones of their speeches have their origin in the unspoken battles of my own youth. The Shavian generation, middle-aged when in the 'thirties I opposed them emotionally, are in the play old people who are being fought openly in the field of ideas. As a result the emotional conflict is stronger than the intellectual argument. This perhaps is one of the play's good points; yet the two strands, emotional and rational, springing from different sources, never quite combine, and this makes for the final lack of punch, one of the play's chief failures. Finally, the sense of threat in the play is stronger than the events — the retirement of James Padley from the college post of Master, even though reinforced by the imminent death that hangs over the daughter Cora — seem to justify. This is surely because the threat really derives in memory from what in the 'thirties seemed likely to be the total annihilation of the coming war.

With the arrival of war, or rather in the first years of war, my two country 'homes' disappeared, both rather typically to become officers' quarters. It was, of course, in the war that country life became associated for me with the almost suicidal melancholy of the mental illness which I have already mentioned. My wartime work was in a somewhat dreary South Midlands countryside never perhaps very beautiful, and for at least a century under continuous threat of ugly urbanization. At the bottom of the garden of the small house in which I was billeted flowed a canal, passing alternately through ugly early Victorian small industrial centres and lush meadowland. Misery in mental illness is hugged close. I well remember walking along those canal banks with murderous thoughts and returning home to reinforce them with a reading of Headstone's pursuit of Wrayburn – Dickens's narrative made more alive for me by my own desperate tramping. The whole countryside, indeed, with its sooty dark red brick houses, its patches of fat, coarse weed that had taken over from decayed habitations, its chapel atmosphere, its wartime lack of motor traffic, had somehow a feeling of what those Midland and Northern industrial towns towards which the barges on the canal were heading must have been in the late eighteenth-century agony hour between a rural and a fully industrial north. It was a countryside still visually that of a feebly flickering cottage industry world. Nevertheless the fact that this countryside had half turned into town more than a century before and got stuck did not prevent my life from being involved in country pursuits. Haymaking, gleaning, poultry feeding, blackberrying, nutting, all the conventional innocently Wordsworthian pursuits that hang around the eighteenth-century mythology of country life, in turn became eaten through for me by the maggots of my neurotic misery. Only gardening and study of wild life were omitted from the unhappiness of this time.

Yet, despite this continuous slow, sweet-sour turning to rotten fruit of my country experience, from my childhood onwards, when in 1955 I decided to resign from the British Museum and give my whole time to writing, my instant decision was for a country life. The decision at the time, of course, came on practical and immediate grounds – need of quiet, absence from telephone (there were no modern amenities in the cottage I leased), economy and so on. None, I think, were as compelling as the lure of the visual aspect of the countryside.

I do not know whether I owe my extreme visual attachment to the English countryside to the conventional influence of the Romantic poetry I have read or to the Norwich School landscape painting I have looked at, or whether to some natural affinity to the lush English scene (and, in lesser degree, to all landscapes with vegetation, though emphatically not to deserts and not to bare mountains); but landscape or animal forms would seem to be the only shapes to which I can respond immediately and without careful preparation. Beside this promise of visual pleasure, the melancholy associations were all forgotten. I think in any case that I can only consciously recall the past in particular incidents and not in general categories. Or perhaps the seductive side of solitude's melancholy beckoned me more than I now remember. Anyhow I moved to the country to live, as it happened quite by myself for considerable periods, for many days at a time seeing no one. And, quite by chance, that country cottage (my present home) was the perfect site for a wild garden. I rented it at first only by the week; I retained my flat in London. The country was only a temporary expedient, as writing had for so many years been 'only a hobby'.

As for the cottage itself, it happened that a friend near by had bought it to save his privacy from being invaded by strangers; it happened to be available exactly when I wanted to move in; it happened to be cheap. It happened to be within reasonable range of London, yet not in a commuting area. It happened to be in a part of England untouched by any memories for me; it happened to be that undulating, yet hardly hilly country which I most love; it happened to be not too near the seaside. It happened in fact to fulfil all my requirements. It also happened to be on the edge of a wood with a much neglected garden. Even if I were not to stay, I must do something, if not to drive the nettles back, at least not to allow them further invasion. With paraffin stoves to fill and oil lamps to clean, I put myself back in the pioneer clearing of my mother's childhood world with a vengeance. It was a role for which neither my London manners and outlook nor my total lack of physical co-ordination nor my innate clumsiness fitted me. Yet I have gone on with it, civilizing the house, eventually turning a clearing in the wild into a carefully artificial wild garden. The symbols underlying my novels have been realized in practice, or more or less realized.

This garden has only once appeared in my writing, in my last novel, *The Old Men at the Zoo*. Once again I introduced the scene without realizing what I was doing; it is geographically out of place (yet only slightly so) but the overtones attaching to it in the fiction gather together and underline all that dialectic, that conflict which has gradually assembled around this symbol in my life and in my work.

To illustrate this it is necessary shortly to relate a section of the novel. The conflict in the narrator Simon Carter, the Secretary of the London Zoo, lies as I have already said, between his exceptional administrative ability and his capacities as a naturalist, particularly in the field of British mammals and, within this range, as an authority on the badger. He is, like most of my central figures, a person of hyper-sensitive moral conscience, sometimes a self-defeating conscience. In choosing between either career he seeks to be altruistic, yet he is too sophisticated not to suspect self-denial as a possible indulgence in disguise. His decision to accept the zoo post represents a triumph for the administrative social side of his nature. In the course of the novel a Natural Park is founded on the Welsh border. He welcomes this Reserve as a possible compromise between his two vocations. He rigidly refuses the career of naturalist on television at which he had once been so successful, for it treats nature study as a means of idle entertain-ment, performs no direct social service, and is gratifying to his vanity. Around the choice of career – a choice in fact between country and town – are gathered then a mass of other moral dilemmas, in varying degree serious or priggishly casuistical. The hoped-for compromise, however, is always the National Park, the cutting into the wild, or the artificially preserved slice of wild life. At moments this compromise appears simply as an escape from the decisions that Simon is unwilling to make in the London Zoo life of political action, at others it seems a health-giving refreshment from the corruption of this active political life. Above all, the escape, good or bad, is centred in the watching of badgers. I have never watched these animals, although I am glad to say that many readers thought the descriptions were taken from experience rather than from the published accounts I used. However, on reading the passages in which I describe badger-watching I notice that I have laid tremendous emphasis on the absolute quiet that must be preserved. This is, of course, an obvious necessity, but I lay far more stress upon it than do the authorities I consulted. Country, once again, as with David Parker's nursery, is associated with quietism, but this time the association is a health-giving, not a death-wishing one. Or so I certainly thought when I wrote *The Old Men at the Zoo*; indeed I chose badgers specifically because they are the least destructive of all our mammals. Save for the occasional small bird or rodent, their diet is largely vegetarian; because of their size they have no enemy in this country and therefore few aggressive-defensive needs. Their only enemy is man, and his hunting of them is wantonly out of proportion to the damage they are supposed to create. In a small island of advancing urbanization they have that peculiar pathos that for me attaches to the large victim of progress.

All this was intended to make Simon's badger-watching – his principal link with the country – a clear positive value; yet as I think again of the course of the story I see that the ambiguities are as great as those attaching to David Parker's nursery garden in *The Middle Age of Mrs Eliot*. Simon's attempts to watch badgers are constantly frustrated at the ill-fated

National Park at Stretton, where he had hoped for his dream compromise. On the first occasion his cowardly betrayal of the unhappy nymphomaniac, Harriet Leacock, brings upon him a comic and ignominious sexual assault instead of the rewarding sight of the gentle, lumbering badgers. On the second occasion the earth is frozen to a deadly, empty stillness. On the third occasion he does in fact see the adult badgers but in an atmosphere of death, for he has just shot Harriet's Alsatian dog, which, unknown to him, has killed its wretched, too fond mistress. On this occasion Simon leaves the badger setts looking forward to seeing the cubs in the coming spring. When that spring arrives not only has the National Park been abandoned but war has broken out. When at last Simon does see the health-giving play of the badger cubs it is only to shoot them.

The circumstances both within the story and its sources which surround this last traumatic episode seem worth analysis. With London besieged and the countryside a devastated battlefield, Simon Carter leaves with the acting director, Beard, to convey some of the animals to a safe country retreat. Beard's motives for the dangerous journey – a wish to preserve some animals for his anatomical researches – are in fact quite alien to Simon's considered reverence for animal life, so that the whole journey is from Simon's point of view a false one. They take a road from London into Essex which I know very well – it is the route out of London which leads more quickly into open country than any other. In fact, after various adventures in which Beard is killed, Simon finds himself, weak and starving, at a country cottage on the outskirts of a wood – presumably in Essex. Yet in fact the description of the wood, as I knew at the time, was taken from the wood by which I now live. The cottage with its Essex country woman and her teen-age son I thought at the time of writing to be invention. But I see now that the cottage is my own, its inhabitants drawn from a family who were then my near neighbours. Nor is Suffolk speech so different from Essex that I had to face this source clearly as I wrote. Certainly the Essex road which Simon travels would be a very long route to where I live now in Suffolk, but it is not an impossible one, and it would be the most completely *country* route possible. Arrived, then, at what is my present home – the cutting in the wild – Simon does in fact see badger cubs for the first time, but only to butcher them to stave off his own famished hunger and that of the woman and her son. When later he eats the badger cub meat he vomits blood and collapses into unconsciousness, the 'nothing' which is the negation of his whole involved humanistic tangle of duties and loves. He has fled the starving, anarchic London mob, the zoo which is the centre of his social conscience, on an errand of false duty only to end by destroying the creature that symbolizes peace and gentleness for him. Unconsciously I had placed the defeat in my own cherished garden in the wild, my own symbol of resolution. The ambiguous symbol when it finally emerged directly into my work proved to be central to my own life.

The opposing values centred around town and country are, of course, many. Progress and tradition; art and nature; good works and the contemplative life; reason and instinct; strained sensibility and sturdy common sense; public and private duties; all these and many other variants can find their expression in the two ways of living. I have argued in the Northcliffe lectures that I gave on *Evil in the English Novel* how important this topographical dialectic has been to the great novelists in the main stream of the English traditional novel. I have also suggested that mere topography has been made to bear a ludicrously heavy load of significance, that inevitably this confinement of the most serious moral values to terms of English geography has increased the natural insularity of our culture. I have also suggested that it has often given depth to the texture of created work and has meant that recollected emotion is fully fused with intellectual and moral design, and I have indicated that for historical reasons the conflict between rootedness and what may be loosely called 'bohemianism', so rich in possible overtones, has become involved, in the English novel, with the defence of a class, the middle class, with consequent restrictions of its breadth of sympathy and of its intellectual range, so acquiring a shrill, ugly defensive note as that class has declined. Thus certain trivial social subtleties have become involved with the whole question of 'the country', and this not without reason, for the social barriers, gross and harsh enough in England anyway, have been and still are grosser and harsher in the country than in the towns. It is quite possible to live in London or a provincial English city outside the class, status fight; even the most determinedly rootless person who goes to live in the country must inevitably become a hermit if he is to avoid the class battle, and even then he will probably find himself placed socially. To protest then against the urbanization of England (or, indeed, of the world at large) thus becomes not only an anti-progressive attitude, in the sympathetic sense that it asserts a refusal to accept the declaredly 'inevitable' consequences of technical advance, but also anti-progressive in a far less sympathetic sense of support for a declining, yet viciously defensive class system. Traditional pieties, stress on the intuitive side of living, attachment to nature, contemplation, private values, are smeared with paltry and temporal loyalties to class mores.

The dichotomy of town and country illustrated in Jane Austen's *Mansfield Park* by the declaredly 'solid' values of Fanny and Edmund Bertram against the witty, declaredly meretricious rootlessness of the London

Crawfords, still repeats itself at times of 'moral crisis' in England. It was the voice of the 'country' that made itself heard so strongly against Edward VIII's proposal of marriage to a *divorcée*. It was after M.P.s had had a week-end objection from their country constituencies that they hardened against the proposal. Such a presentation of the country-town moral dichotomy reduces it, of course, to a petty level of a largely fabricated moral indignation, concerned with the preservation of a particular class system. To take sides with the 'sound' country gentry against the 'unsound' clever, café society aristocracy of London, or vice versa, as we are always asked to do when a member of the royal family makes an unusual choice of lover, is to be asked to take sides with Tweedledum against Tweedledee. Unfortunately in England over the centuries this petty aspect of the conflict between country and town values has become so ascendant that it is difficult to remember that the dichotomy is a serious one, and lies at the roots of civilized man's dilemmas.

Thus all espousal of the 'country' cause in England becomes ridiculously suspect of class arrogance or snobbery. Therefore I find myself questioning my own choice of the wild garden as a symbolic resolution. That I have traced its origin in my father's childhood makes it curiously suspect, for from my father comes the whole ambiguous story-telling talent that I have developed. Am I attached to it because it comes from the one claim to gentility that my ancestry allows me? Does not its very name, 'wild garden', suggest large artificial plantings in great estates beside which any 'wild garden', if indeed it ever existed outside his fantasy, in my father's Scottish home could be no more than a suburban shrubbery? Do I perhaps detect in myself the same snobbish claims as suburban Miss Woodehouse of Hartfield? In my childhood I heard so often the word 'common' thrown about as an adjective of abuse that I still feel the need to find some sort of unpleasant correlative for it – to pretend to gentility by magnifying a childhood symbol, that is surely 'common'. Am I 'common'? So deep are the class overtones of my upbringing (and that of the greater part of all Englishmen of all classes, I think) that I cannot even satisfactorily put forward the 'clearing in the wild' derived from my mother's childhood, to offset the 'wild garden'. Of course this colonial, pioneering image has all sorts of sterling moral values to oppose to the declining world of my father, but are they more genuine? We have come to know that the descendants of colonial pioneer stock in Australia, or South Africa or Canada, assert their primitive moral strength, their harder, more spartan virtues, largely as a cover for their harder, more primitive, more single-minded attachment to the accruing of material wealth; and so, in fact, with my mother's family it is. And this, without mentioning another even less attractive hard simple-mindedness shown by the whites in South Africa – a simple, pioneer attachment to the cruelties of apartheid, for instance. A snobbish class upbringing fortified by a Marxist education in history – most history teaching at Oxford in my day, even the most right-wing teaching, accepted some sort of Marxist class interpretation of social evolution – all this has made me highly conscious of the social overtones of any values I propose. This suspicion of snobbery in country living, along with other less trivial objections to country values that I have already discussed, has served to undermine the force of the wild garden as a positive value and has contributed to the negation by which Simon Carter comes to kill and eat the badger cub in a scene uncommonly like the author's own chosen home.

This unconscious location of a fictional climax in a real setting raises the whole question of the novelist's visual picture of the geographical setting of his work, and not only the geographical setting, but the time span, and the relationship of the characters. How far do these answer to any similar patterns in the 'real' world. How far is the fictional world merely a more or less considerable distortion of the real?

I am a person who easily visualizes life – my own life and other people's lives – in terms of maps, time charts and genealogies. I think this is the most marked effect upon me of my education. I failed to learn any mathematics, but the order and pattern that I might have achieved from them were built deep into my preferred subjects of geography and history. If I remember at some moment a particular object that I have seen, say the Blue Mosque in Istanbul, then the natural tendency of my mind, if unchecked (of course it is usually checked by other thoughts), is to place this building in relation to other famous Istanbul mosques that I have seen, and these in turn I see visually on what I remember from the whole map of Istanbul in my Blue Guide. If I am tired and idle the picture will begin automatically to expand. Istanbul will appear on a map of Turkey beside the other Turkish towns I have visited, which will in their turn acquire visual details. This map will also be marked with the towns I failed to see, in feebler pictures of details that I have only read of – Trebizond from writings or remarks of Rose Macaulay, Lake Van from a French novel that was laid in that area, and so on. On the edges of my consciousness, waiting to slide into vision, if I am unoccupied or tired, is a whole world map, appearing something like those demographic charts in which densely populated areas are heavily studded with black dots, Antarctica largely a blank. My map, however, has black dots of real experience and grey dots of imagination and, in between, varying shades to mark literary associations, historic events, the home towns of people whom I have met when they were travelling abroad, and so on. Thus on my mental map the London area is a black splodge, Provence richly black, Antarctica (the scene of many of my ice fears) a heavy grey, Tehran lightly marked by my view of the airport in the early morning hours, overshaded because it is the residence of an old friend, cross-shaded by the word Mussadiq and his pyjamaed form (which fades by association into the pyjamaed form of another captive 'evil' figure, Dr Mabuse). Above this world map with its overlays or shadings and collections of dramatis personae, time spirals upwards so that each place too has its historical chart either dating personal experiences or bringing into mind its historic past. I cannot have, as perhaps a scientist could, any spiral of the future. The sheer weight of my obsession with history, however, has given my imagination at times a furious hunger for some prophetic counterweight which science-fiction can only partly assuage.

Marseilles, which I knew well in adolescence and have later visited periodically for a few nights when motoring in France, has dates clearly marked above it on the map in my mind: 1931, 1935, 1937, 1938, 1946, 1948, 1952, 1956, 1959, 1962. It may well be that some of these years are inaccurate, but so they are fixed in my memory. Each year carries the names or the facial expressions or associative objects of different companions – to analyse the different shorthands by which people make their impact upon memory would prove, I suspect, embarrassingly revealing of one's purely physical feelings for them. Over all hangs a general picture of the Cannebière looking up from the Vieux Port and the Vieux Port quarter as it was pre-war; somewhere on the edge lies Corbusier's apartment house on its stilts and the zoo with a Polar bear with sores that I remember from my earliest visit. Around the hazy edge I can detect some pictures of Marseilles seen in a television documentary about Simone Weil, and more clearly Mr Meagles talking to Miss Wade at the opening of *Little Dorrit* (but not the more famous scene of Rigaud in prison which somehow has no geographical setting for me). Somewhere far off is Dumas's Château d'If covered with a peacock butterfly that settled on my hand there. The chains of association, geographical, historical, or purely associative, are no doubt much the same as most other people's. I suspect that the rigid map-time-chart shape of my memories is less general. It is the only automatic discipline that my historical education has given me and it can be conveniently called 'educated memory'.

This educated memory plays an essential part in all the conscious preparations I make when I am writing fiction. It is of obvious importance in controlling and maintaining a broad-canvassed narrative like *Anglo-Saxon Attitudes*. It also perhaps accounts for a too mechanical regularity in the parts of my books – for example, the balancing of each character's public behaviour by an analogous marital relationship pointed out by Mr Francis Hope in his review of *The Old Men*

at the Zoo. As a result, the conscious artistry I am able
to contribute to my novels is far more evident in their
general composition – methods of narration, pro-
portions of narration, all the preparatory labours, in
fact – than it is in the actual writing, where a more
primitive, less educated memory, which I shall discuss
later, tends to take over.

Some contrasting examples of the maps and time-
charts that I constructed in my imagination in composing my four novels may say something of the effect
of this type of educated memory upon fiction writing.

Hemlock and After is the most conditioned by one
piece of actual geography, and, paradoxically, the
least related in general to my own personal memory
map. One of the characters (not the central character)
in this novel was more directly taken from life than
any other I have created, so directly that I was unable
to divorce the fiction from reality to the extent of
changing the habitation in my mind. As a result the
whole novel spreads out from an actual place, and in
my mind as I see the book even now there is a clear
map of England, and of the particular parts of England
in which every action of the book, every character's
location is marked. Yet when I began to write the
novel and saw how firmly fact and fiction were identified, I had, for obvious reasons, deliberately to smear
the transfer so that everywhere in the book the places
were out of their original siting. Thus it was before
quite another church than the St Albans Abbey of the

book that I originally saw Ron's failure to pick up Eric; Mrs Craddock, compounded from one or two other real people, I did not picture at all as living in Esher; Bernard Sands, in so far as he was drawn from myself, lived in a house totally unsuited for so eminent and successful a man, and so on. The smudging process I carried out in various ways – St Alban's was deliberately and mischievously chosen as the most improbably respectable place for such a prank (I have liked to think that other Rons and Erics have sought the Abbey precincts, perhaps with more success, as a result of my smudging); Bernard's location outside London was made deliberately vague with results of the kind I have already discussed in the incident on the Downs, so that geographically he wanders at random through my own memories without regard to place; on top of my original models for Mrs Craddock and Eric (not, in life, in any case, at all connected) was superimposed an American woman and her son met briefly in Esher many years before, and a memory of their house on a hot afternoon combined with the woman's nationality to give the swampy, Miss Magnolia touch that I wanted, to increase the absurdity of Celia's character as I had compounded it.

I am not sure that any of these deliberate disguises of place are losses, nor that readers will find the geographical sense of the book any less convincing. But for me, when I re-read *Hemlock and After*, there was a baffling sense that all the distances suggested in the

novel – Eric's bicycle rides, Mrs Curry's assignations
with Hubert Rose, Bernard's solitary walks, even the
arrival of the distinguished crowd from London at
Vardon Hall – were seen in a distorting mirror, because
I had still the first imagined map before me. I am inclined to believe that this plays some part in the quality
of the characters of the novel. Since the geographical
locations were deliberately chosen at random to
disguise the original ones they had few overtones of
memory for me and none that came directly out of the
created characters; the psychological connections
between the various characters seem to me attenuated,
almost snapped by the distorted geographical distances. I am inclined to think that this may have added
to the somewhat one-dimensional, sharp-edged, card-
like effect of the characters – people without pasts (or
with only the sketchiest of pasts), isolated islands.
This is luckily consonant with the satirical purpose of
the book anyhow; and, since I do not remember being
at all worried by the geographical changes as I wrote
them, I may be seeing effects where they do not exist.
Certainly the visual appearances of the places – Esher,
St Albans and so on – which I selected arbitrarily were
necessarily sharply in my mind because they had been
so consciously chosen. Nevertheless I am sure that
the novel would have been a fuller, richer narrative
and a more significant moral argument if I had
developed the character of Bernard Sands's principal
antagonist, the architect Hubert Rose; this could only

have been done by dramatizing his sexual life, which in turn depended upon his obsession with a now dead relationship with his absent sister. All this I told in a few short sentences. To have brought it to life I should have needed to have felt the impact of the character's past life, and, floating in a geographical void, Hubert never got sufficiently clearly placed on my imaginary geographical map to acquire any existence in time.

If I am right in finding fault with the 'map' of *Hemlock and After*, it is no argument against founding novels either upon real geography or upon imagined geography, only against shifting from one to the other, or rather to a map chosen arbitrarily for reasons unconnected with artistic creation. It is, I think, only one more example of the disadvantages of accepting characters too immediately from real life, before they have undergone the moulding of imagination or of amalgamation with other pieces of reality.

The geography of *Anglo-Saxon Attitudes* is quite different. Although as I wrote I could see from whom certain characters had been derived, no character was consciously based on reality as I composed the book, and no character came from one single person, although some were amalgamations in which the external characteristics of one component were finally all too evident. Unlike Bernard Sands in *Hemlock and After*, or even more Meg Eliot, the central figure, Gerald Middleton, had almost no roots buried in me or in my life. As a result the places were chosen primarily for their social and emotional aptness in relation to the characters. They sprang to life, indeed, with the characters. A map of London with the characters placed exactly, both at home and at work, was clearly before my imagination all the time as I composed; every movement, every character was visually tracked in detail on this map in my mind, that is to say by a continuation of visual pictures (some so strong, as of Gerald walking in the park, that they forced themselves into written narrative), some in personal shorthand, others in visual pictures of routes marked on the map. The places abroad to which Gerald went were more deliberately chosen for their aptitude to characters and events, although, of course, I had been to them and could visualize them in some detail. The map of *Anglo-Saxon Attitudes* first grew from certain streets and squares selected from my own permanent personal mental map of London, rather as, on those French Metro maps, by pressing a button your route is plotted out in electric lights. Spokes of the lighted route then began to shoot out over England, into East Anglia for the archaeological discoveries, down the river to Inge's house, farther westward to Dolly's cottage in the Cotswolds; finally out of England altogether, to Aigues Mortes and Arles, to Merano, to Elsinore, and, finally, last sign of Gerald's freedom, to somewhere I have never visited – to Mexico. In this way the scenes are fused occasionally with my personal emotions (as, for example, in Gerald's motor trip in

France with Dolly which follows many sentimental journeys of my own) but more often only with my own social participation – I have known rather than felt the Earl's Court of Frank Ramage, I have known rather than felt the Knightsbridge of Gerald and the Hampstead of his daughter-in-law Marie Hélène, I have seen many times but not participated in the coming together of these worlds at Fortnum and Mason's as they do in the book. Merano, the scene of the retirement of the old Shavian D'Annunzio-worshipping actress-suffragette Lilian Portway, and of her brutal death, was chosen because that arcaded, mountain-dominated, claustrophobic town has a stronger feeling for me of decayed causes of all kinds (Tridentine, Habsburg, etcetera) than any place I know. Incidentally, I feel now that the invasion of the French spiv, Yves Houdet, into the old woman's Merano retreat was a foresight of the more brutal and least attractive sides of 'miracle' Western Europe breaking up all the old claustrophobic haunts of forgotten feuds and dead history. Once again, as in country versus town, my sympathies are ambiguous; certainly Yves himself suggests all my doubts about the ruthless and corrupt side of the new 'miracle' world.

Two locations in the book remain rather unsatisfactory to me even now. Ingeborg Middleton, Gerald's Danish wife, was conceived as a Bavarian. For a number of personal reasons, however, I did not wish to underline the German aspect of the character; these reasons were reinforced by the chronology of the novel which demanded that Gerald should court her during the 1914 war. Courtship of a German girl at that date was improbable and would in any case have introduced a host of irrelevant emotions. Gerald's position as a scholar of Viking history made connections with Scandinavia likely. Everything was set for Ingeborg to become a Dane. Yet how uneasy I was with the decision I can see from my emphasis upon her emotional inheritance from her Bavarian grandmother. Many readers, unfamiliar, I suspect, with Scandinavia, have told me how exact the character's nationality is; but I doubt if Scandinavian readers think so and I suspect that for once the aggrieved are right. I know Denmark somewhat, and from books very well, but my picture of the scene at Elsinore where Gerald proposes had to be made from the memories of a single visit. It lacks elbow-room. Since it marked the introduction of Ingeborg into the novel, it strongly influences the development of her character. I think that she might have developed from a successful grotesque into one of my best-imagined characters, had I been able to 'feel' rather than to 'know about' her background.

It is difficult to justify such a distinction. In the first place, all the characters in this work are built up as social observations, and the vertical time-charts that stand above their geographical locations on my imaginative map were necessarily derived from historical knowledge rather than from personal experience. In the second place, even though, as I am sure, such historical social constructs are imaginatively more transposed into living beings if they can be informed with personal memory as well, it is nevertheless true that a past constructed for a character from documents will often be more accurate than one derived from memories. Thus since I know Elsinore only a little I felt forced to find out from old guide books what was the condition of the castle and whether it was open to the public in 1918; as a result the factual account of this scene of Gerald's proposal to Inge is very exact. An equally important scene with Gerald's mistress Dolly is laid in Aigues Mortes, a town I have known rather well over a long time, even indeed roughly at the date, 1930, when the scene is supposed to take place. Despite my frequent visits I made a major mistake in describing the subject of a statue. Yet I am quite sure that the scene at Aigues Mortes is more living than that at Elsinore, and the character of Dolly received life from it, even though it is not so vital to her as the Danish background is to Inge. Yet when I say this, do I mean any more than that I know my picture of Aigues Mortes to be capable of wide expansion from my own memory, and that I also know that my description of Elsinore has exhausted almost all that I remember of the place? Do I supply additions from my memory to the Aigues Mortes scene as I read it? Would a reader who knows neither place notice any difference in the quality of the two descriptions? It is this kind of relation of life to art that biographical information seeks to illuminate.

The other location that troubles me also concerns Inge. I do not remember why I placed her house when she is separated from Gerald at Marlow, nor do my preparatory notes for the book, which are very full, reveal this. I think it likely that I chose Marlow partly on social grounds as a rich comfortable near-com-muting area. I am sure that I did not find in Inge an embodiment of the conflicts I have described as belonging to the concept 'country'. For this reason she is permitted no serious gardening and could not live in the 'real country'. Yet why, in all this rich near-commuting Thames area, should I have chosen Marlow? I do not care for the Thames Valley at all, yet if I were forced to live there Marlow would be my preferred town. Perhaps this is the measure of my wish not to be 'unfair' to Inge. The only firm association I can make with Marlow lies in Shelley's residence there. Shelley's life has always been of obsessive interest to me. It would be easy, I suppose, to find some connection between the hysteric, falsely sweet view of life held by Inge and some aspects of Shelley's character. Marlow, indeed, is where Shelley's hysteric imagination led him to tell Peacock of the supposed visit of the land agent from Wales. But I'm afraid such a connection would be invented, for Shelley, for all his defects, is a much-loved hero figure in my mythology. Inge was emphatically not seen as heroic; she has only the pathos of a comic Brünhilde. Marlow is entirely dead in the novel, and I think I must have chosen it for arbitrary and inadequate reasons.

The whole geography of the book seems to me a little ostentatiously documentary; but then this is perhaps inevitable in a novel whose central theme demands the constant fusion of private and public life. In any case the vertical lines of past history that stand above the geographical locations are more important than the locations themselves in a book that is concerned with the effect of the past upon the present. It is inevitable, too, that a novel the whole shape of which is organized, and organized very formally, out of the memories of Gerald Middleton (who is in no way a part of myself) should draw principally upon the shaded areas on my map that denote associations derived from reading and knowledge rather than from experience. The most 'thought' of my novels and the least 'felt', I feel for *Anglo-Saxon Attitudes* least now that it is written and done with.

Yet one good effect comes from this carefully constructed map of places and parts that are little fused with my own feelings; its exactitude (one can always check knowledge, one can seldom check past experience) and its freedom from my own emotions have allowed the characters to make connections one with another, to develop, that is, in terms of art rather than of experience. During the composing and writing of *Anglo-Saxon Attitudes* however preoccupied I was with any one character, I was always closely aware of the total map, the location at that time of other characters. As a result the awareness of each character of the others, the interrelationships (positive and negative) are always maintained. Each character at all times seems to have an apprehension of the existence of the other characters. Thus, if it is an over-documented map, it is also a map in the round, almost a globe in the way that each point connects with all the others.

Only in *The Middle Age of Mrs Eliot* have I filled a novel with myself. Yet this does not affect the geography as much as I should have expected. The map of Meg Eliot's world is in no sense the same as my own, although, of course, once again, as in *Anglo-Saxon Attitudes*, the places of Mrs Eliot's life light up on my own mental map and, as they do so, take on something of my own memories. Although Meg is much drawn from me, I have never known the economic and social circumstances either of her prosperity or of her deprivation. The externals of her life as a rich married woman are drawn from an amalgamation of two women that I know, but her home in Lord North Street sets her somehow a little apart from either of them, as I wanted her to be. When I came to fix the location of the charity organization Meg helps to run, I visualized a youth club where I had attended a B.B.C. rehearsal of a play of mine. Yet

it was not the building itself that came to my mind but
rather a memory of a story told me by a social-worker
friend of mine, of coming out of a youth club to find
some small, rather raggedly dressed children scratch-
ing the paint of his car. As I thought of Meg I felt that,
from my own sensations as I heard this story – reactions
very different from those of my professional friend –
I had known exactly how Meg would have reacted in
the situation. From this momentary reaction I was led
into her emotions about poverty, distress and so on.
With these I could work back to her behaviour on the
committee and, of course, forward to her feelings
when she herself lost much of her social privilege.
I was let in sideways, so to speak, to my own emotions
had I been an amateur social worker.

These moments of total identification, as I planned
and wrote, came again and again, and they nearly
always arose from a geographical memory. I have
already spoken of the identity of Meg's crucial Far
Eastern visit with my own; indeed the seeds of the
book were sowed while I was in Bangkok. I have also
suggested the way in which her brother David's
nursery was located where my friends had lived, and I
have conjectured why this should have been so. But I
think that perhaps I set David's nursery in Sussex for
an additional reason. As I have never had a sister, I had
to imagine the relationship of Meg and David. Yet I
have a niece not too much younger than I am, to whom
I have always been devoted and with whom I spent

much time in my youth. My earlier happy memories of association with her are of those parts of Sussex where Meg and David drive together during their rediscovery of their childhood closeness. It may be that this was an impelling reason for the lighting-up of the Sussex part of my map, or perhaps the two memories fused: the one of happiness at my friend's home with its subconscious undertone of resentment could be soothed by the other of my niece which had no such hidden conflicts. Yet my relationship with my niece, if unalloyedly happy, has avoided deep emotions, and so was well chosen, if my guess is right, to lead into the climax of the novel where Meg rejects the cosy but deadening intimacy into which she and David are falling.

The geography of *The Old Men at the Zoo* was, of course, chosen for me when I decided on the London Zoo for my setting. The memories and emotions roused by the theme of the 'administrative' side of the novel came from my experience when working at the British Museum and in the Foreign Office. They are quite unrelated, of course, to the emotions I connect with the London Zoo, which have grown from childhood onwards into the wild-life dilemma I have already described. Simon Carter, the narrator, is the fusion point for me of these two sets of memories, as he is for the conflict between administration and nature study. The geographical map, then, is almost a unity of place; the narrator Simon leaves the area of the zoo and his near-by home only five times in the long novel. I referred above to his flight from starving London and its tragic ending in what I now see to be my own garden. The geographical position of an earlier deceiving paradise of the book – the Natural Reserve at Stretton, intended by Dr Leacock to replace the zoo – was determined by more banal practical considerations; it had to be chosen from any of the few areas of considerable unpopulated or little populated land left in Great Britain. In selecting the Welsh border I was influenced partly by these practical considerations, partly by my personal feelings. My personal choice would have been East Anglia because I prefer its scenery to any other in England, but its terrain would hardly have proved suitable for any but a very limited number of species. There were left the Welsh Marches, the Northern Marches, and the West Country. I love Northumberland as I do Herefordshire and Monmouthshire. I somewhat dislike Devon and have so far refused ever to visit Cornwall. I indulged myself then by eliminating the West Country: 'Exmoor and Dartmoor,' Dr Leacock tells us in his broadcast, 'have gone the way of the South Downs' – so was my own boyhood country disposed of in a parenthesis – 'I did not think it necessary to bring to your notice the miraculous housing developments, the grand factory sitings that private enterprise has provided in New Taunton, West Exeter and Plymouth Drakeville.' The enormities of unchecked private building speculation by 1970 may shock Dr Leacock's sense of country planning, but they satisfactorily saved me from having to write with tenderness about the West Country, a part of England that I dislike. Between the Scots border and the Welsh there was little to choose, but the latter's climate is more clement and I know it better. So I put Lord Godmanchester's enormous estates in the Welsh Marches. Mr Raymond Williams, an authority on this area, in his review of my novel pointed out that Hereford had no such sleazy 'pub frequented by tarts and Irish layabouts' as I described. He may well be right, although my experience of cathedral towns suggests that most of them do have their 'less reputable sides', as Hugh Walpole depicted in *The Cathedral*. What perhaps needs explaining, or at least further explaining in view of my many descriptions of real sources, is how little such a mistake of fact seems to me important, how I feel no need to make any such preliminary research as would avoid it.

In writing novels I have never been able to place much importance upon the distinction between real and imagined. A novelist, it seems to me, makes as much or as little use of the real world as he needs to project his vision of life. Mr Raymond Williams clearly feels that the mistake about the location of the pub in some way invalidates the picture of life given in the whole novel, or rather, I should say, that shakiness in such a fact suggests a general shakiness of knowledge and comprehension of the world the novelist lives in and from which his novels ultimately derive. Professor Frank Kermode in his book *Puzzles and Epiphanies* includes a very interesting review of *The Middle Age of Mrs Eliot*, but here he attacks from the opposite side to Mr Williams. It is what he thinks to be my excessive care for 'reality' that disturbs him. 'Yet it seems,' he writes, 'that Angus Wilson himself thinks that they (his people) matter only in so far as they are "real". This is curious; in the earlier novels, and most damagingly in *Anglo-Saxon Attitudes*, there is an evident clash between fantasy and neo-realism.'

I am not really able to meet either of these charges because I do not, in fact, care for exact realism, either as Mr Williams thinks I should or as Professor Kermode thinks I should not. I have never felt called upon to declare allegiance to either fantasy or realism. They proceed from two different levels of my imagination and without their fusion I could not produce a novel. However, if I must choose between two necessities I should consider the 'real' as the less essential. The tendency to confuse the novel with sociology seems to me the weakest aspect of modern English fiction. Perhaps I have been classed with such neo-realists because I happen to be fascinated by atmosphere and have built it up by accumulation of details. For this I depend, indeed, upon eye and ear as any reporter would do, but what matters to me is what my imagination does with the reports of my eyes and ears, not in the faintest degree the reports themselves. That I have also been interested in writing novels about man in society in a decade when some other English novelists have been laying stress on the social novel, has perhaps associated my novels with theirs, but the connection seems to me flimsy. The purpose of my book about Zola, who notoriously depended upon exact fact for the stimulation of his imagination, was to show that what mattered was the nature of his imagination, not the facts that stimulated it.

This, in short, seems to be the whole case about this so-called conflict between fantasy and realism: some people need the stimulus of reality more, some less; some more at some times, some less at others. Correlative reality can nag an author when the imagination is flagging, as legal exactitude clearly nagged at George Eliot with the construction of *Felix Holt*. But for the most part novelists seek what exactitude they need and no more. Miss Murdoch in her fine novel, *The Bell*, felt the need of exactitude about the methods of raising sunken bells; I do not imagine she was too concerned with any real counterpart to her religious community. Novelists take what they will where they will and when they will. There is, it is true, a connecting point between the real world and the creation made from it, even in novels so little 'realistic' as *La Tentation de Saint Antoine*, *The Lord of the Flies*, *The Confessions of a Justified Sinner*, or *La Rôtisserie de la*

Reine Pédauque. The joints or hinge-points of these two worlds are often the details upon which novelists fuss and bother themselves for exactitude : details of speech forms, or street numbers, or costume, or machine constructions, or the exact brand names of consumer goods. Often I find that I have fussed only later to dissolve the 'realities' that I have spent so much time confirming. But if the 'real' detail nags too greatly it suggests, I think, either some exhaustion of the creative imagination, as with George Eliot in *Felix Holt*, or some over-selfconsciousness about the purpose of creative imagination, as with M. Robbe-Grillet in a novel like *Le Voyeur*, or, as with a great part of the less distinguished serious English novelists today, a confusion between novel writing and sociology for which perhaps they would have been better suited.

It is here, in fact, at this hinge-point where the real world is being split up and dissolved and remade into fiction, that the educated memory which I have been describing, the memory, which in my case has been historically trained to make time-charts and maps and a whole complicated plot organization, meets with and is fed by the uneducated memory of images and humour and unrelated incidents or names or faces. This second memory, coming in my case from an earlier part of my life, is what gives vitality to the novel, makes the words flow, the incidents happen, gives to the constructed plot of time and place I am building up with my educated memory any of the irony, absurdity, *macabrerie* and pathos that make my fictional world my own and not just a cleverly (or insufficiently cleverly) constructed novel-shape. To analyse this deeper, free level of memory is difficult indeed, for either the associations spring from too deep a source to be dredged up, or to describe even a short passage would require such a profusion of personal detail to explain each sentence that every explication would be of far greater length than the text. This is no doubt, as has been recently often remarked, why Dickens's most characteristic genius, his humour, has so daunted all his many analysers.

In examining my own free memory I can see only one *outside* separable influence. As a child I was much with my brother next in age – thirteen years old when I was born. He was a youth of exceptional histrionic powers, strangely combining sharpness of wit and tenderness of heart, extremely effeminate, with deep powers of creation that were never fulfilled. His wit and his fantasy have both strongly influenced the texture of my free imagination, giving it an unusual quality of severely moral chi-chi and camp. To him also I owe the pervasiveness of the feminine in my work – the strength of the female characters, their invasion of every part of my books, the affectionate mockery with which this invasion is treated. For the rest – the grotesque, the macabre, the purely absurd, the sadistic, and the compensatingly pathetic – I can find no external influences. They seem to me, as they burst into my memory when I write, invading and distorting the hard outlined, tightly constructed 'real' world I have invented in my preparatory schemes, to be 'myself', something innate finding expression in images, dialogue, incidents, and even just words.

I think that I can best illustrate this vital stage of novel-writing, when the free memory takes over from the educated memory, by citing two passages from stories I have written about small boys. In the games of the first, Johnnie, I have almost, I think, reproduced the hodge-podge fantasy of my free memory. In the reverie of the second, Rodney, an older boy, I have tried to suggest such free memory being shaped into narrative, constructed, not like Johnnie's for his own diversion and delight, but to justify, to exploit, to satisfy conscience. The memory here is being educated for a purpose.

'His [Johnnie's] imagination was taken by anything odd – strange faces, strange names, strange animals, strange voices and catchphrases, all these appeared in his games. The black pig and the white duck were keeping a hotel; the black pig was called that funny name of Granny's friend – Mrs Gudgeon-Rogers. She was always holding her skirt tight round the knees and warming her bottom over the fire – like Mrs Coates; and whenever anyone in the hotel asked for anything she would reply, ''Darling, I can't stop now. I've simply got to fly" like Aunt Sophie, and then she would fly out of the window. The duck was an Echidna, or Spiny Anteater who wore a picture hat and a fish train like in the picture of Aunt Eleanor, she used to weep a lot, because, like Granny, when she described her games of bridge, she was "vulnerable" and she would yawn at the hotel guests and say "Lord I am tired" like Lydia Bennet. The two collie dogs had "been asked to leave", like in the story of Mummy's friend Gertie who "got tight" at the Hunt Ball, they were going to be divorced and were consequently wearing "co-respondent shoes". The lady collie who was called Minnie Mongelheim kept on saying, "That chap's got a proud stomach. Let him eat chaff" like Mr F.'s Aunt in *Little Dorrit*. The sheep, who always played the part of a bore, kept on and on talking like Daddy about "leg cuts and fine shots to cover"; sometimes when the rest of the animal guests got too bored the sheep would change into Grandfather Graham and tell a funny story about a Scotsman so that they were bored in a different way. Finally the cat who was a grand vizier and worked by magic would say, "All the ways round here belong to me" like the Red Queen and he would have all the guests torn in pieces and flayed alive until Johnnie felt so sorry for them that the game could come to an end.'

In contrast here is Rodney: 'Four years ago I still could know the seashore, especially the summer seashore of purple sea anemones, of ribbon weed clear like coal tar soap, of plimsoll rubber slipping upon seaweed slime, of crab bubbles from beneath the rock ledge – but now I have grown up – thirteen years old, too old to make my bucket the Sargasso Sea, too old to play at weddings in the cliff cave, too old to walk with handkerchief falling round my calf from a knee cut afresh each day on the rocks. Now there is only the great, far-stretching sea that frightens me. If I were like other boys, I should be getting to know the sea by swimming in it, treating it as my servant, somewhere to show off my strength, to dart in and out of the waves like a salmon, to lie basking on the surface like a seal. Mummy and Daddy and Uncle Reg can move like that. At one time they tried to teach me to join them, but now they have given me up as hopeless. I can watch their movements and wish to imitate them, but when I am in the water I am afraid. I am so alone there, its great strength is too great, it draws me under. I can lie on the beach and dream – I am Captain Scott watching the sea leopard catch the awkward penguins; I am the White Seal as he swam past the great, browsing sea cows; I am Salar the Salmon as he sported in the weir; I am Tarka the Otter as he learned to swim downstream; above all nowadays I am lying in the sun on the deck of the Pequod with the Southern Cross above me. But there always comes the moment of fear – Captain Scott has dread in his heart as he reaches the Pole too late; the White Seal grows up to fear the hunter; Salar the Salmon must dart from the jaws of the conger eel; Tarka lies taut beneath the river bank as the hounds breathe overhead; on the Pequod is heard the ominous tapping of Ahab's ivory leg. Even in my dream I must be afraid, must feel unprotected.

'The sea swings away from me now, brown and sandy in patches, but without light, grey and cold. It heaves and tosses and lashes itself into white fury, as it crashes and thunders against the breakwater. It flies into a mist that sprays against my cheeks. But always, however the waves may rush forward; tumbling over each other to smash upon the beach, the sea swings towards me and away from me. I am sitting upon a raft and the calm, level water is swinging me so, back and forward. It is the Pacific Ocean everywhere, clear and green. Over the side of the raft I can see deep, deep down to strange, coloured fishes and sea-horses and coral. I am all alone, "alone on a wide, wide sea". Mummy and Daddy have gone down with the ship, spinning round and round like the Pequod. See! She sinks in a whirlpool and I am shot out, far out, alone on this raft. The heat will scorch and burn me, "the bloody sun at noon", and thirst and the following sharks. Don't let me be alone so, don't let me think of that. But now the sea is moving, violently, wildly in high Atlantic waves. I am lashed to a raft, the sea is swinging me roughly, up on the crest so that the wing of the albatross or the seahawk brushes my cheek, raucous screams are in my ears, hooked beaks snap at my eyes, and now down into the trough where the white whale waits. Mummy and Daddy have gone down with the ship. It crashed and broke against the glass-green wall, the name Titanic staring forth in red letters as it reared into the air. Mummy's black evening dress floated on the surface of the water and her shoulder showed white as she was sucked down. But I am left alone, tied to the raft, numbed, frozen, choking with the cold, or again, as it sails relentlessly on towards the next floating green giant, dashing me to pieces against ice as I fight with the ropes too securely tied!'

These two fantasies of Johnnie and Rodney, with their mixture of literary and personal memories, very faithfully reflect, so far as I can recall them, my own imaginings at the same ages. Both pre-date the historical training which was to organize my fantasies in the sort of way I have called 'educated memory', the basis of the composition of my narratives. But though in the growth of my imagining over the years from childhood (Johnnie) through boyhood (Rodney) to maturity (educated memory) the sequence is direct, in the making of novels the process is altered. Rodney's imaginings with their purposeful form (usually ethical, often ambiguous, closely related to semi-conscious demands of the ego) come first. They are then shaped and controlled into plot, proportion, scene, time span and so on by the 'educated memory'. And lastly, when the whole book is composed and the form is strongly enough built to resist fragmentation, the batteries of Johnnie's 'free' memory are let loose upon all this shaped, tendentious material to give life, imagery, wit, absurdity, pathos, and so on in the actual writing. It is in this most primitive fantasy-making that my own sources of feeling are most completely loosened, giving often, from depths of a once rather starved affection, passages that sometimes embarrass critics by their sentimental or theatrical tone; or again pleasing or shocking readers by the unloosed sadism which finds its expression in elaborate flights of humour, of absurdity, or of the macabre.

Out of the struggle of these three different levels of imagination comes more or less successful art. Kept to themselves, the fantasy levels of Johnnie or of Rodney might become respectively a 'camp' gossip or a confidence trickster. And indeed gossip, confidence trickster, actor, or door-to-door salesman are only some of the things which the 'free' (Johnnie) or the self-concerned (Rodney) fantasy-maker may grow into.

We novelists are in the world, as Thomas Mann well knew, of Tonio Kröger and Felix Krull. Novels are lies, novelists disreputable people in their basic nature. It is perhaps to combat this that the novelist has worked so hard at the moral, 'education for life' power that has won him Dr Leavis's approval. Gossip, confidence trickster, huckster, or novelist, all are kept in action by the power of narrating. I have suggested in a lecture to the Association of Professors of English that this narrating power may also be (artificially) separated from the novelist's other components. I am certainly conscious myself of a purely narrating power that is loosed in me, once the moralist and the composer have given way to the process of writing, to the free imagination. It is the pure horse-power of the narrator that keeps me physically able to write on from day to day, to wake in the morning and continue writing the book despite all the claims of personal letters or of the newspapers, claims either horrible or pleasant. To say that the narrating voice asks, 'and what next?' so insistently that no exhaustion, worry, lust, or happiness can withstand it, is not to narrow the novel to a simple story level (Foster's, 'oh dear, yes, the novel tells a story'), for *Ulysses* or *Finnegans Wake* or *Nightwood* also demand, 'What next?'. Particularly is this lowly esteemed, near-disreputable narrating art needed to meet exhaustion, for in novel writing are combined two opposite qualities that pull the writer apart. He must, as he writes, draw upon the depths of his free memory, that is to say he must be a passive vehicle allowing images, scenes, absurdities (every kind of vision and sound) to flow into him; at the same time, if his novel is to be more than a cosy 'total recall' he must be ready to interpose actively, strongly, to force the flowing material into the previously composed shape. A hair's breadth one way and the novel sags with too heavy a weight of sensation, a hair's breadth the other and its life has been strangled from it. It is not surprising that there are so few perfect novels. That there are so many decent ones is not a little due to the 'narrator' who bridges the passive free fantasy-maker and the active artist.

The word is inevitably out at last, for no amount of delving into the autobiographical sources of novels, no analysing of the processes of creation, no revealing of the ambiguities of the writer's aims, can finally explain the making of a novel. Nor is an analysis of the craft of the novel a true statement of what the novelist believes that he is doing when he writes his book. It is unlikely that a novelist can account for his impulse to make a work of art in language that is wholly rational. In part because to do so would demand an accurate memory of a momentary experience whose coming is without that heralding which alerts the memory – its significance is all in its after-effect and none in its coming. In part also, of course, it is difficult to isolate the novelist's creative impulse as clearly even as the painter's or the composer's for, unlike a painting or a concerto, a novel acquires so many additional significances – social, psychological, moral and so on – as it takes shape. The 'pure' aesthetic critic (not at all the same as the 'pure' critic) is a rare bird today and therefore to be cherished; but he can never, I think, be wholly happy with so mixed a form as the novel.

Equally, a true novelist with all his mixed motives, can never be really satisfied with an aesthete's novel like *Marius the Epicurean*. Nevertheless, if only in protest at the paramount importance placed upon the supervening significances of the novel, moral, social and so on by critics and novelists alike today, I should wish to end this book by registering my own experience that the impulse to write a novel comes from a momentary unified vision of life.

In my original conception of *Hemlock and After*, for example, I saw Mrs Curry, obese, sweet and menacing, certain in her hysteric sense of power that she can destroy a good man, Bernard Sands; and because my vision is primarily ironic, I saw Bernard painfully thin, bitter, inward-turning, defeated and destroyed, not, as Mrs Curry thought, by her knowledge of his private life but by his own sudden impulse of sadism as he witnessed the arrest in Leicester Square. A momentary powerful visual picture of a fat woman and a thin man. The whole of the rest of the novel, for good or bad, is simply an extension needed, as I thought, to communicate this very visual ironic picture to others. In this way I could analyse the impulse that started all my novels.

The novels, in fact, *are* those moments of vision. No didactic, sociological, psychological or technical elaboration can alter that significance for the novelist himself. Like any other artist's, the novelist's statement is a concentrated vision; he aims as much as any symbolist poet or impressionist painter at seizing the 'stuff' of life and communicating it totally; but, unlike the others he has chosen the most difficult of all forms, one that makes its own discipline as it goes along. We can never hope for the perfection, even with a Tolstoy, that other arts can achieve with a Piero della Francesca or a Bach. But any serious novelist who tries to describe aspects of his work and does not announce this vision as his central impulse is either playing down to some imaginary 'plain chap' audience or has forgotten his original true inspiration in the polemics of moral, social or formal purpose. Everyone says as a commonplace that a novel is an extended metaphor, but too few, perhaps, insist that the metaphor is everything, the extension only the means of expression.

FOR THE BEST IN PAPERBACKS, LOOK FOR THE

In every corner of the world, on every subject under the sun, Penguin represents quality and variety – the very best in publishing today.

For complete information about books available from Penguin – including Puffins, Penguin Classics and Arkana – and how to order them, write to us at the appropriate address below. Please note that for copyright reasons the selection of books varies from country to country.

In the United Kingdom: Please write to *Dept JC, Penguin Books Ltd, FREEPOST, West Drayton, Middlesex, UB7 0BR.*

If you have any difficulty in obtaining a title, please send your order with the correct money, plus ten per cent for postage and packaging, to *PO Box No 11, West Drayton, Middlesex*

In the United States: Please write to *Dept BA, Penguin, 299 Murray Hill Parkway, East Rutherford, New Jersey 07073*

In Canada: Please write to *Penguin Books Canada Ltd, 2801 John Street, Markham, Ontario L3R 1B4*

In Australia: Please write to the *Marketing Department, Penguin Books Australia Ltd, P.O. Box 257, Ringwood, Victoria 3134*

In New Zealand: Please write to the *Marketing Department, Penguin Books (NZ) Ltd, Private Bag, Takapuna, Auckland 9*

In India: Please write to *Penguin Overseas Ltd, 706 Eros Apartments, 56 Nehru Place, New Delhi, 110019*

In the Netherlands: Please write to *Penguin Books Netherlands B.V., Postbus 3507, NL–1001 AH, Amsterdam*

In West Germany: Please write to *Penguin Books Ltd, Friedrichstrasse 10–12, D–6000 Frankfurt/Main 1*

In Spain: Please write to *Alhambra Longman S.A., Fernandez de la Hoz 9, E–28010 Madrid*

In Italy: Please write to *Penguin Italia s.r.l., Via Como 4, I-20096 Pioltello (Milano)*

In France: Please write to *Penguin France S.A., 17 rue Lejeune, F-31000 Toulouse*

In Japan: Please write to *Longman Penguin Japan Co Ltd, Yamaguchi Building, 2–12–9 Kanda Jimbocho, Chiyoda-Ku, Tokyo 101*

The Woman in Black   Susan Hill

Young Arthur Kipps had no suspicion that Eel Marsh House guarded the memories of a pitiful secret – nor did he understand that the black-robed woman who inhabited its shuttered rooms exacted a terrible revenge. 'Authentically chilling' – *Sunday Times*

A Handful of Dust   Evelyn Waugh

From a decaying country estate to the decadent savagery of thirties London society, and finally to a living hell in the Brazilian jungle … With cold comedy and lacerating irony, Waugh's masterpiece traces the break-up of a marriage.

Animal Farm   George Orwell

'The creatures outside looked from pig to man, and from man to pig, and from pig to man again; but already it was impossible to say which was which.' Orwell's fable of a revolution that went wrong has become the classic satire of the twentieth century.

The Old Devils   Kingsley Amis

This Booker Prize-winning novel about Alun Weaver's and his wife's return to their Celtic roots is 'vintage Kingsley Amis, 50 per cent pure alcohol with splashes of sad savagery' – *The Times*. 'Crackling with marvellous Taff comedy … this is probably Mr Amis's best book since *Lucky Jim*' – *Guardian*

Him with His Foot in His Mouth   Saul Bellow

A collection of first-class short stories. 'If there is a better living writer of fiction, I'd very much like to know who he or she is' – *The Times*

The Anglo-Saxon Attitudes

The grotesque idol discovered in Bishop Eorpwald's tomb has scandalized, mystified and inspired a whole generation of scholars. As a young man Gerald Middleton was involved with the dig. Now an eminent historian, he is none the less haunted by a sense of failure both as a man and as a scholar.

In *Anglo-Saxon Attitudes* – considered by many to be Angus Wilson's masterpiece – a gripping detective story of archaeological fakery combines with the portrait of a man compelled to face the truth about himself and his marriage, family and professional life.

'Angus Wilson's brilliant and ambitious novel is about the conscience as it worries two generations of a middle-class family ... And here lies the great originality of Mr Wilson as a novelist and the richness of the book. Its moral seriousness is matched by the comic explosions of our tradition' – V. S. Pritchett in the *New Statesman*

'No other English novelist of his generation has offered as complete and detailed a portrait of English society ... His ears missed nothing, not a single nuance. They captured, time and time again, the sound of the way we live now' – Paul Bailey in the *Observer*

Hemlock and After

For Bernard Sands, the novelist, great liberal and humanist, the setting up of a writer's colony at Vardon hall is to be the climax of his distinguished career. But Bernard has influential enemies, and life is further complicated by his wife's mysterious illness and his own homosexual affairs. Writing with dazzling originality and insight in this, his first novel, Angus Wilson ensures that Bernard's liberal ideas, public and private, are put to the test.

'A very remarkable achievement . . . Mr Wilson is one of the most gifted and original writers of his generation' – Jocelyn Brooke

'His novels are capacious, taking in an ever altering social scene, and their veering from naturalism to the fantastic, and from brittle wit to the tenderest of sentiment are the often daring narrational tricks which provide his unique hallmark' – Ronald Blythe in the *Guardian*

'An outstanding book' – John Betjeman

The Old Men at the Zoo

'Each new novel by him is an adventure, opening up strange perspectives of the heart and mind to the reader's alerted and alarmed inspection' – *Sunday Times*

In the offices of London Zoo Simon Carter, the new Secretary, is enmeshed in power games with his colleagues. Into this disciplined, civilized atmosphere breaks the cataclysm of atomic war. As the novel develops into a chilling imaginative vision of the apocalyse, blending myth, symbolism and fantasy, Angus Wilson emerges as one of the most influential political satirists of the twentieth century.

'He is more talented than six ordinary novelists put together' – Gavin Ewart in the *Evening Standard*

'He wanted his novels to *encompass* life, not merely to be *about* life. He was more concerned to move his readers than to dazzle them. Though at times ... he does both ... a great novelist' – Rose Tremain in the *Guardian*

No Laughing Matter

This exhilarating, panoramic novel charts the fortunes of the Matthews family, a group of unconventional, middle-class Londoners, from the First World War to the 1960s. Theatrical, brilliantly mixing parody and pastiche, it explores history as farce and superbly captures the complexity of family relationships and tensions.

'*No Laughing Matter* draws its strength not from its cunning technique but from its unerring sense of what made England tick between the two worlds wars.' – Paul Bailey in the *Observer*

'One can truly say that Mr Wilson omits nothing. One hears again each popular song of the period, sees again the hair-dos and the clothes, listens to the remarks about the remaining politicians, the stage-plays, the leaders of fashion, the tendencies in the arts' – *Sunday Telegraph*

The Middle Age of Mrs Eliot

Meg Eliot, the wife of a successful barrister, leads a very privileged life. To assuage her guilt, she occupies her time on charity committees helping those less fortunate. Reluctantly uprooting herself, she escorts her husband on an extended tour abroad and is suddenly, shockingly widowed. Gradually her own strength and immense courage is channelled into rebuilding her life as a woman on her own.

This major novel, winner of the James Tait Black Memorial Prize, is a supremely sensitive portrayal of human perseverance and determination in the face of tragedy.

'What makes this novel tower above the fiction of a decade is the full-length presentation of Mrs Eliot herself . . . She may be one of fiction's great female creatures' – *Daily Telegraph*

'A work of deep compassion but unstinting moral examination' – Malcolm Bradbury

and forthcoming:

As If By Magic
Late Call
Setting the World on Fire
Collected Stories